# Landmarks of France

# Landmarks of France

text by Jean-Jacques Delpal
translation by Michel Gresset

LIBRAIRIE LAROUSSE
17 rue du Montparnasse, Paris

*Editorial office :* M. F. Vaudois et A. Renaut-Dard
*Art directors :* F. Longuépée et H. Serres-Cousiné
*Iconography :* A. M. Moyse
*Proof-reading :* N. Chatel et B. Dauphin

Larousse ISBN 2-03-523104-3
Newnes ISBN 0-600-35786-4

ENTLE FRANCE, so dear to poets, has shores on three seas and one ocean; unrolls its varied landscapes under pearl-grey or deep-blue skies; is patterned by diverging rivers, and upheaved by big, rounded hills or high, steep mountains. The crossroads of Western Europe and a nearly perfect hexagon, it can be seen as a natural entity on small-scale maps. However, this is a deceptive appearance, as the limits of France are the effect of history as much as of geography. It was only in 1860, with the annexation of the Comté de Nice and Savoie, that the old nation born out of Île-de-France was given its definitive borders. The largest European state after U.S.S.R., France is a harmonious blending of regions once independent or at least autonomous, some being former dukedoms or even kingdoms. Now one fatherland, hewn out by kings and by the republic, it is nonetheless a many-faceted country, made of various climates, landscapes and kinds of men. And yet there are innumerable shades and gradual transitions which tone down the contrasts without concealing the infinite variety in which lies the essence of its charm.

The French landscape is all but monotonous. Large plains covered with waving corn alternate with vine-grown hillsides, green valleys with dried-up moors, rugged coastlines and cliffs with long beaches of pale golden sand. Even water has its own moods, whether nimble, torrentuous, or quiet, slowed down by bends or spread into motionless lakes and ponds. The lazy Saône flows into the headlong Rhône, the Seine is serene, and the Loire whimsical.

France has metropoles like Paris, the Lille-Roubaix-Tourcoing conurbation, Lyon and Marseille; yet it is mostly made of medium-sized towns, big *bourgs*, and countless villages. Even though industrialized as all modern countries are, it nonetheless retains a pronounced rural character. With the exception of the largest cities, the French habitat mirrors the various climates, natural resources, needs and customs of the population; it is a model of integration within the natural setting. Vine-growers' houses, big and small farmhouses, cottages, Southern *mas* or bourgeois dwelling-places are almost always part of the local landscape. The high slate roofs are part of a grey sky whereas the round tile heralds the Mediterranean. The masons of yore used either the white chalk, the severe granite or the tractable brick, all of which nowadays are too often replaced with the sad, nondescript concrete. Noble architectural landmarks bear witness to the trends of their times as well as to a continuous evolution, but the romanesque art of Burgundy differs from that of Languedoc, and the gothic cathedrals, though sisters, are not twins.

An old tendency to centralize has always been the cause of many revolts even while the nation grew steadily around Paris, the siege of power and the capital at the centre of a spiderweb of roads and railway tracks. Although arbitrarily divided into *départements* under the Revolution, France remains a conglomerate of regions large and small, which retain their idiosyncracies, their own sense of the past, their language or their dialect, or at least their local accent. The old names of Touraine, Quercy and Alsace are sweeter to one's ears than Indre-et-Loire, Lot, and Bas- and Haut-Rhin. In the twentieth century, the French people are still predominantly Bretons, Normans, Picards, Savoyards, Alsaciens, Bourguignons, Angevins, Auvergnats, or Corsicans. And they still belong to their towns and villages.

## Historical landmarks

*Before the Roman rule began with the battle of Alesia (52 B.C.), the area now covered by France was inhabited by gaulois peoples who had few contacts with, and were rather hostile to one another, but who were united by a common language and by a form of civilization. After its conversion to Christianity, the galloroman world gave way under the thrust of the Francs at the beginning of the Vth century. Four centuries later, Charlemagne set up a huge empire which was put to pieces by his inheritors. In 987 (Hugues Capet), the Capetians began their patient work toward the unity of France, and settled in Paris for*

*good. They gradually prevailed over their highly independent vassals and put their lands together. Il was not easy: through the play of marriage and inheritance, England almost ruled over half of the territory.*
*After the English were thrown out at the end of the Hundred Years' War (XIV-XVth centuries), Louis XI tamed his wild vassals and united Burgundy and Anjou to the Crown. And Henry IV brought Béarn to France after the tragedy of the Wars of Religion. The feudal lords rebelled under the Fronde, but were curbed by Louis XIV, an absolute sovereign. During the reign of the Sun-King,*

*France was in a constant state of war, but it was made larger by the annexation of Franche-Comté and part of Flanders.*
*Even though the Revolution felled the monarchy and proclaimed the republic, it carried on the former's centralizing work. After the First Empire (1804-1815), the kings came back on the throne, but the republic was reestablished after the riots of 1848. However, Louis-Napoléon Bonaparte managed to have himself proclaimed emperor (1852-1870). Ever since the failure of the Commune (1871), France has been a republic. It had found its present borders in 1860, when Savoie and the Comté de Nice both chose to joint it.*

*Lutèce was a small but important village located on the Île de la Cité. The Romans turned the village into a city and it spread to the left bank (the public baths of the Hôtel de Cluny, the arenas). The city's name was changed to Paris in the IIIrd or IVth century. It became the capital of the Franc kingdom in the beginning of the VIth century, and it had many ups and downs until the end of the Xth century, when Hughes Capet established the royal residence there. During the reign of Philippe*

*Auguste (XIIth-XIIIth centuries), Paris grew a great deal. Many churches and monuments were built and the city became famous thanks to its university. Henri IV was one of Paris's great urban developers and the city continued to grow pushing back its all-too confining walls many times. During the XVIIIth and XIXth centuries, rural areas shrank due to land development. By the end of the First Empire, Paris had 700,000 inhabitants and more than 1,000 streets. Under the Second Empire, Baron*

*Haussmann, the great urban developer created the large avenues. Paris incorporated the surrounding villages and its influence spread to neighbouring departments. Paris was occupied from June, 1940 until it was liberated in August, 1944. Starting in the sixties, the city changed further due to largescale construction projects, the building of the riverfront road and the R.E.R., the opening of the Centre Pompidou-Beaubourg complex, and the renovation of Les Halles, the old downtown district.*

5

# Paris

THE LARGEST CITY IN FRANCE, sometimes charged with despotism, Paris is a department of its own, the well-known "75" to be seen on the registration plates of automobiles and on the zip code of the post office. It is both the head and the heart of the nation, a devouring metropolis, and a living museum. Both glorious and hard-working, the city of Paris has inspired thousands of poems; no single formula can sum it up, however. The ring road or *périphérique* now hems in an ancient town bristling with concrete buildings; in fact it holds together several cities whose lineaments change with the times of day and the seasons. An inventory would consist in dozens of churches and museums, towers of the past and towers of the future, the monuments of the kings of France and the Pompidou Centre, noble, bourgeois or popular *quartiers* or districts, large, congested thoroughfares, market-streets and old-fashioned squares. Officially, this octopus of a city is divided into twenty *arrondissements,* but Parisians do not really care for administrative borders. They live and work in as many towns, or even big villages as there are *quartiers.* In spite of the constant changing and mixing inherent in present day life, the latter have kept their peculiarities and their advocations: do not confuse Montmartre and Pigalle, the Latin Quarter and Saint-Germain-des-Prés, the Opera and the Palais-Royal, Auteuil and Passy!

The finest avenue in Paris is still the ample bend of the river Seine, which is crossed over by thirty-four bridges and foot-bridges with names evocative of history: Pont Marie was built in the XVIIth century; Pont de la Tournelle is watched over by the statue of Saint Geneviève, the protectress of the city; Pont d'Arcole is named not after a town in Italy, but after a young rebel of the 1830 revolution; Pont-au-Change reminds one of the jewellers and changers of the XIVth century; the first stone of Pont-Neuf was laid by Henri III; the sumptuous Pont-Royal was built by Jacques Gabriel after the plans of Hardouin-Mansart; the metallic Pont Mirabeau inspired Guillaume Apollinaire, etc. And then, on the *quais* or embankments, there are the antique-dealers, the second-hand booksellers called *les bouquinistes,* the bird-merchants, the flower-market... The long list of bridges and *quais* recalls the wedding of the capital with the river which attended its birth.

## Lutèce, an island in the bends of the Seine.
The escutcheon of the City of Paris, on which is also to be seen the ship of the mariners and boatmen of yore, bears an image of the river Seine embracing two islands one of which, the Île de la Cité, was the cradle of the capital. The city grew in concentric circles around the original nucleus of Lutèce: the remnants of the old walls, the *boulevards extérieurs,* the *péri-*

*phérique* and even the suburban *couronne* or crown can be seen developing like the streaks of a cut tree-trunk. Once made lively by the traffic of many river-boats, the Seine now unrolls its ribbon of brown water under the heavy barges, the tug-drawn convoys and the *bateaux-mouches.* Even though its embankments have been turned into utilitarian thoroughfares, and it is polluted, the Seine has retained a powerful charm, and it looks fresher every spring when it reflects a light-blue sky. Napoléon III called it "the main street between Paris, Rouen and Le Havre". It is still the meeting-place of second-hand booksellers, opinionated fishermen and lovers, as well as of the Eiffel Tower, the Tuileries gardens, the Louvre, the Institut de France, the Conciergerie and Notre-Dame. You cannot be truly familiar with the city without loitering along the *quais* which still belong to day-dreamers, and without lingering on the prow or the stern of the twin isles or on the Concorde bridge, which commands an admirable vista.

Parisians, even though they live in a *quartier,* belong either to the busily commercial Right Bank or to the intellectual Left Bank. Another division is between residential West and popular East, whereas the Centre is now the seat of many companies, offices, stores, cinemas and theatres. In daytime it is lively, often even jammed; at night, some places are almost dead: the city of shopping and business

*Two of Paris's familiar sights: the bewitching waterworks at the foot of the Eiffel tower* (opposite); *basking in the sun on Place du Tertre* (above).

8 is deserted when the lights are put out in the shop-windows. Whether they are huge urban areas or still village-like, the quartiers of Paris have joined the capital and its history one after the other. Some are very old in terms of their association with Paris: the Latin Quarter and the Châtelet, for example; others were born out of the urbanization process of the XVIIth, XVIIIth, and XIXth centuries: the Marais, the Palais-Royal, the Île Saint-Louis, the Observatoire, the Gobelins, the Champs-Élysées, the Étoile, the Ternes... Others are former villages caught in the spiderweb of the expanding city: in the 1860's Grenelle and Vaugirard, Belleville, La Villette, Montmartre, Auteuil and Passy were annexed and have kept a provincial charm in spite of the traffic jams and the pouring of concrete.

The river and the wide boulevards opened during the Second Empire lay out itineraries within the dense network of the city, which can find breath in its parks and gardens (Parc Monceau, Buttes-Chaumont and the Tuileries gardens on the right bank, the Luxembourg gardens and Parc Montsouris on the left bank, with Bois de Boulogne and Bois de Vincennes flanking the whole conurbation). Yet it is difficult to recommend any definite plan for a visit. In Paris, the threads of Ariadne end up in knots and entanglements, stretching from monuments to museums and from department stores to luxury shops, taking the visitor abruptly from the cobble-stones of Montmartre to the neon signs of Pigalle, from old stones to developing areas. Balzac has written that Paris is "a true ocean: there you can always find an unexplored spot, an unknown retreat, pearls, monsters, something unheard of". It is a capital that cannot be seen at first sight.

**Notre-Dame, the Parish of French History.** Most of the monuments of Paris can be found within the limits of the walls built by the Fermiers-Généraux (1784-1796), of which only a few rotundas and toll-houses are left. The Île de la Cité, anchored to the city by bridges, is all but crushed under the heavy buildings of the XIXth century. The Sainte-Chapelle is still walled in by the enormous Palais de Justice, whose colonnade overlooks the Place Dauphine; but thanks to the new parvis Notre-Dame emerges admirably. Notre-Dame is both the cathedral of Paris and "the parish of French history". It was built between 1163 and 1330, remodelled during the XVIIth century, and restored in the XIXth by Viollet-le-Duc. There are more stately edifices in the world; some are higher, others more richly decorated; but none is more harmonious

*At the heart of the capital, on Île de la Cité, stands Notre-Dame, one of the masterpieces of Gothic architecture.*

than this Gothic masterpiece of the Middle Ages, about which Paul Claudel once said: "It is not only an edifice; it is a person." Notre-Dame is a history-book: it keeps the memory of Saint-Louis, who brought back the Holy Relics to it; of Philippe le Bel, who rode into it; of Henry VI of England, who was crowned King of France in it; of Bossuet's orations; and of the crowning of Napoléon. In 1945, the Te Deum of victory was heard, and in 1970 the state obsequies of General de Gaulle were held there.

Protected by its famous square towers which are part of the symbols of the city, Notre-Dame first comes to sight with its portals, its bold flying-buttresses, and its spidery chevet. The nave and the aisles, fringed with innumerable chapels, are steeped in a chiaroscuro where the light issuing from the huge roses (some of the stained glass windows date back to the XIIIth century) appears to melt.

The "Great Relics", among which is the crown of thorns brought back by Saint-Louis, are only visible on Lent Sundays, but the fabulous treasure of the cathedral is on show in a vestry built by Viollet-le-Duc — a splendid museum open to the public. The magnificent grand organ by Clicquot still booms with its six thousand pipes, and every Sunday afternoon, the best organists play Bach, Pachelbel, Liszt and Dupré in the largest concert-hall in France (nine thousand persons can attend, fifteen hundred of whom can stand in the galleries).

The precious XIIIth century Sainte-Chapelle is a gem which unfortunately is enchased in an ill-fitting case. It was built on the order of Saint-Louis. It is beautiful when seen from the outside, although it cannot be viewed from any distance. Inside, two chapels are superposed. The upper one is steeped in a dazzling, unreal light coming from the blue and red windows upon which are narrated over a thousand scenes from the Scriptures. The series is a rare set, full of incomparable variety and verve.

A pedestrian bridge crosses over from the Cité to aristocratic Île Saint-Louis, a world of its own, away from the tumult and the traffic. The island was formed by the reunion of two islets which had been deserted until the XVIIth century. It bears no famous monument, but its XVIIIth century *hôtels* or town-houses are superb, and its embankments have a charm of their own.

### The Arch of Triumph, the colossus of the Place de l'Étoile.
The right bank stretches all the way from the old villages of Passy and Auteuil to Père-Lachaise, an immense

cemetery in which one can take an unusual walk, to the popular Faubourg Saint-Antoine, and on to the Fort de Vincennes, a fortified palace with another Sainte-Chapelle — a flamboyant one. High above the rodeo of automobiles, the Arch of Triumph overlooks the Place Charles-de-Gaulle (which Parisians will still call by its old name, the Place de l'Étoile). Begun under the initiative of Napoléon I and finished under the reign of Louis-Philippe, the monument has a huge high relief sculpture representing the victories of the First Republic and of the Empire on each of the four sides of its grand arch. The upper platform allows a superb view, while an eternal flame burns on the Tomb of the Unknown Soldier, one of the victims of World War I.

To the west, the Arch of Triumph enframes the slender buildings of the new business center of La Défense, the parisian Manhattan which can be reached on the R.E.R., a "supermetro" running under the capital from one suburb to another. To the east, the famous "Marseillaise" carved in stone by Rude faces the perspective of the Champs-Élysées, "the most beautiful avenue in the world". Running over nearly two kilometers, the avenue begins as a row of cinemas, cafés with pavements, luxurious shop-windows and commercial galleries; in its lower part, it runs through gardens where Marcel Proust played as a boy, and where edifices are hidden under the foliage of trees. The gardens have hardly changed since the construction of the Grand- and Petit-Palais, which are both typical of the "Belle Époque" with their ambitious dimensions and their heavy deco-

*The Conciergerie* (above), *which overlooks the Pont-au-Change, has retained its fine medieval air throughout the centuries. The remains of the palace of the Capetian kings, it was long used as a prison and many were its famous inmates from Ravaillac the regicide to Queen Marie-Antoinette. Now part of the Conciergerie is used as a museum and it reveals its gloomy past from room to room, whereas the other part of the stately building belongs to the adjacent Palais de Justice.*

*The Opera* (opposite), *also called "the temple of music and dance", was designed by Charles Garnier in one of the busiest districts in Paris, the grands boulevards. It is the most original building left by the Second Empire.*

*The Arc de Triomphe* (right), *ordered by Napoléon I as a tribute to his own army, and inaugurated by Louis-Philippe in 1836, watches over the Champs-Élysées.*

rations. A large thoroughfare flanked with wide pavement car parks, the Champs-Élysées have kept their lordly air in spite of the unceasing flow of automobiles. Originally meant as an extension of a walk drawn by Le Nôtre in 1670, the avenue is still one of the symbols of parisian luxury. However, it has turned somewhat austere with the arrival of automobile makers, air travel companies, big banks, and office buildings. The Lido and Fouquet's are still there, but the Claridge is gone — the only large hotel on the "Champs" — and so have many shops.

Today, the only true luxury street left is the Faubourg Saint-Honoré, where the windows of the antique dealers, "grands couturiers" and stylish hair-dressers can be seen almost next door to the Palais de l'Élysée, a sumptuous XVIIIth century palace originally owned by the Marquise de Pompadour, Louis XV's favourite mistress, and now the residence of the Presidents.

The Champs-Élysées end at the Place de la Concorde, the largest square in Paris, at the centre of which the obelisk, a gift from Egypt, stands at the crossroads of two admirable vistas. The Place itself, at once rigorous and sumptuous, was designed between 1753 and 1775 after the plans of Jacques-Ange Gabriel. Two XVIIIth century buildings with high colonnades enframe the rue Royale (where Maxim's is) at the far end of which can be seen the façade of a Greek temple — the Madeleine church, built in the XIXth century. For the sake of symmetry, on the other bank of the river a corinthian colonnade was added to the Palais Bourbon, a composite building which is the seat of the Chambre des Députés.

Between the Concorde and the Carrousel, an arch of triumph built in 1806-1808, stretch the walks, the lawns and the flowerbeds of the gardens of the Tuileries, strewn with innumerable statues, and upon whose terraces stand the Musée du Jeu de Paume (impressionist paintings) and the Pavillon de l'Orangerie. As one walks away from the French gardens, which were redesigned by Le Nôtre in 1664, one crosses lawns ornamented with statues by Maillol, and one reaches the huge palace of the Louvre, an historical monument and a truly universal museum.

**The Louvre, an example of an architectural puzzle.** The endless palace of the Louvre, bearing the arms of several sovereigns, shows an apparent unity although it consists mostly of additions and juxtapositions. A real architectural puzzle, its construction was begun again and again over the centuries: the Cour carrée was begun under Henry II, the Galerie du Bord de l'Eau dates from the time of Catherine de Médicis, the colonnade from the time of Louis XIV; and the wings on each side of the Place du Carrousel were built by Napoléon I and by Napoléon III. Only Leningrad's Ermitage can match this daedalus of a museum, the fabulous collections of which cover all times and cultures, and occupy 225 galleries, rooms and cabinets. Among the best known pieces are the Venus of Milo, the Winged Victory and Mona Lisa, Rembrandt, Rubens and Tintoretto, the jewels of the Crown — and particularly the Régent, a 137-carat diamond from India. The Louvre illustrates the whole span of the history of art, from the old Egyptian Empire to Delacroix, Corot, Courbet and Carpeaux.

The stately colonnade of the Louvre, which was designed by Perrault, is a little overbearing for Saint-Germain-l'Auxerrois, a composite church built at the height of

14

the Gothic period but marked with several later architectural styles. The north side borders Rue de Rivoli, a long traffic artery begun in 1804 with arcades permitting a glimpse of the Palais-Royal, a lovely XVIIIth century architectural unit onto which the Comédie-Française theatre seems to have been grafted. There, the mysterious galleries and the large, quiet garden are a nook out of time, which seems to be peopled with innumerable ghosts. Nearby the traffic roars along the Avenue de l'Opéra, a large commercial thoroughfare which is one of the favourite haunts of Japanese tourists. It leads up to an enormous *pâtisserie*, Charles Garnier's Opera. "No style at all... It is neither greek nor roman", Empress Eugénie is supposed to have said when she was shown one of the largest theatres in the world. "Your Majesty, it is Napoléon III", replied the architect.

On the south side of the Louvre are the embankments or *quais,* with all their bent trees and the shops where one can buy birds, dogs, cats and monkeys—down to the Place du Châtelet, at the angle of which can be seen the unusual sight of the Tour Saint-Jacques, a flamboyant spire without a church. Next is the Place de l'Hôtel-de-Ville, formerly Place de Grève, the scene of many executions.

**From "Beaubourg" to Le Marais.** The Centre Pompidou, better known as "Beaubourg", is in sharp contrast with the neighbourhood around it. A few years ago, the inhabitants of the square formed by Châtelet-Halles-Rambuteau-Saint-Merri were the dumbfounded witnesses of the construction of a fantastic combination of metallic beams, tubes, and rods painted in bright blue and tomato red. The huge futurist skeleton was a shock to some, who called it "Pompidou's monster" (the centre was named after the President who instigated it). Once finished, however, the Centre became an object of curiosity attracting as many visitors as the most venerable monuments in Paris. The capital can be said to have assimilated Beaubourg as it did the Eiffel Tower. Parisians no less than tourists have come to like the pedestrian area at the foot of the Centre, and they keep crowding the largest museum of con-

*From the Arc de Triomphe at the Etoile to the Louvre, Paris can boast of one of the finest vistas in the world (preceding pages). In between its two ends are the spectacular Place de la Concorde, harmoniously composed with Italian-style fountains, the Luxor obelisk, statues, and colonaded buildings; and the arch of triumph of the Carrousel (below), which is reminiscent of the famous Roman arches with its rich bas-reliefs. The palace of the Louvre comes last as one walks down from the Etoile. It was the royal residence for centuries, before housing one of the most fabulous museums in the world. The room of the Caryatids (opposite, left) houses the huge statues of Jean Goujon as well as masterpieces of Greek sculpture.*

*Shown above are the elegant façades of the Louvre and the garden of the Carrousel.*

temporary art in the world, with its exhibits and its huge library. The pivot of the renewal of the central part of the capital, the "monster" is connected with the remodelled Halles district, a modern development built over a gigantic underground station (R.E.R., metro, S.N.C.F.).

The town-hall or Hôtel de Ville, rebuilt in the style of the Renaissance in the XIXth century, conceals the classical façade of Saint-Gervais-Saint-Protais, a church which is the boundary of Le Marais, the largest protected architectural area in France. At once aristocratic and popular, saved at the last minute from total degradation by an ambitious program of renovation, the Marais is truly a museum of XVIIth century civilian architecture, with about a hundred architectural masterpieces. The heart of the area (once a marsh — hence its name, Le Marais) is the Place des Vosges, a large square edged with buildings erected upon the order of Henry IV. A wonder of harmony, the Place des Vosges was the haunt of the *literati* under the Ancien Régime. Madame de Sévigné was born there and lived nearby, in a house which is a masterpiece of Renaissance architecture, even after being remodelled by François Mansart during the XVIIth century: it was called the Hôtel Carnavalet, and it is now the seat of a museum devoted to the history of Paris from Henry II to the present.

On the edge of the Marais, a winged genius of Liberty can be seen perched on top of the frail "Colonne de Juillet", named after the Revolution of July 1830, and raised at the centre of a big roundabout the name of which refers to quite another revolution in quite another month of July: the Place de la Bastille, where the prison-fortress stood, which was stormed by the mob on July 14, 1789, and immediately razed to the ground.

**Montmartre, the Eiffel Tower, and the Boul'Mich.** Way up north, the hill of Montmartre watches over Paris. On top of it is the Sacré-Cœur, a strange Roman-Byzantine basilica whose dome offers the finest panorama over Paris and its region, and whose construction began in 1826 on the highest point in the capital. At once a village and a belvedere, constantly flooded by tourists, Montmartre pretends it is independent and will keep its paved streets, its old houses, and even its own acre of vineyards where more or less folkloric harvests are held each year. Always crowded in the summertime, the Place du Tertre is

never more picturesque than when the sorry painters of souvenir-pictures leave it alone; the Butte, with its deserted steep streets and its long, lonely flights of steps, should be explored on a fine, clear winter day.

In terms of height, though, the Eiffel Tower is easily the winner over the Sacré-Cœur: the "shepherdess of clouds" (Apollinaire) is over 1,000 feet high if one includes the TV antenna. Erected by Eiffel between 1887 and 1889, the iron tower stands across from the panoramic terrace of the Palais de Chaillot, a huge complex which houses the Musée de la Marine, the Musée de l'Homme, and the Musée des Monuments français. Behind the tower (which was once loathed and is now well-beloved) can be seen the stately École militaire, one of the great monuments of the XVIIIth century. To the east, beyond a wealthy area, the vast Esplanade des Invalides is limited by the 680-feet long severe though harmonious front of the noble Hôtel des Invalides, with a most elegant dome rising from the middle of it. A true labyrinth with its ten-mile long maze of corridors, the Hôtel was built by Libéral Bruant and Hardouin-Mansart in the 1670's as an abode for the victims of war. It is now the Musée de l'Armée. Napoléon I lies under the dome, the chancel of which is shared by the church of Saint-Louis, also called the Chapelle des Soldats (several of the Emperor's companions are buried there). At the edge of the Esplanade, the district called the Faubourg Saint-Germain is not very lively; uniting a group of about one hundred hotels of the XVIIIth century, it is now the seat of several Ministères, of the Premier's offices, and of several Embassies.

The church of Saint-Germain-des-Prés, which is partly romanesque, has a remarkable gate tower. However, the tourists seated at the tables of the "strategic" Café des Deux Magots seem less drawn to it than to the perpetual movement of a young, many-colored crowd. Once a quietly bourgeois area, Saint-Germain has become the parish of existentialists and jazz-fans, and is now one of the liveliest districts in Paris, the centre of night life all year round. If one wishes to take a leisurely stroll along the streets with the antique-dealers and fashion shops, one must come in the morning: it is only after the latter is well begun that the Flore, Lip, and Castel quiet down.

The wide Rue de Rennes, opened in the XIXth century, used to take the visitor to the old Gare Montparnasse until the latter was replaced by a modern development at the

edge of which stands a 660-feet tower which is elegant but hardly in harmony with traditional Paris. Boulevard Saint-Germain is the link between Saint-Germain-des-Prés and the old Latin Quarter, for eight centuries the seat of learning and protest. Centered around the Sorbonne, the student area stretches from the Luxembourg gardens to the Seine along Boulevard Saint-Michel, or cosmopolitan "Boul'Mich". The Latin Quarter includes the almost medieval, now pedestrian section around the Saint-Séverin church, a masterpiece of flamboyant Gothic architecture, and of Saint-Julien-le-Pauvre and Maubert, with the picturesque Rue Mouffetard, which is still the haunt of hoboes, nearby.

Surrounded as it is with suburbs often called dormitories, Paris is now a city to which one goes to work or for entertainment, and less and less a city where one lives. It is the seat of the State and it houses the Ministères, the Embassies, the Departments of the Administration and the big companies. It is also, however, the finest shop-window in France. Almost all of its districts have several "in" boutiques, but the luxury and semi-luxurious items are to be found on the Champs-Élysées, along Faubourg Saint-Honoré, Avenue de l'Opéra, Rue de Sèvres, Quartier Saint-Germain-des-Prés, and Boulevard Saint-Michel.

People sleep heavily in the periphery and in the areas only devoted to business. The "gay Paris" is centred around the Champs-Élysées, Saint-Germain-des-Prés and Pigalle, while islands of light will last all night long in Montparnasse and in the Montparnasse area.

*The Place des Vosges* (left) *is a haven of rest away from urban tumult. Brick and stone townhouses frame its peaceful garden.*

*The dome of the Invalides chapel* (right) *was built according to the strict laws of classical art. It was consecrated to the memory of the Emperor Napoléon I, whose ashes were buried under it.*

# Ile-de-France

AN EXPANDING NEBULA at the edge of which "new" towns have cropped up (Évry, Marne-la-Vallée, Cergy-Pontoise), the Paris "crown" is a medley of low-rate council flats, towers, cottages, and industries. Wealthy in the west and populous in the north and east, the suburbs are highlighted by a few beautiful parks and can boast of one famous monument: the basilica of Saint-Denis, the prototype of Gothic cathedrals and the necropolis of kings. Like Notre-Dame, the church built by Abbé Suger was in danger of falling down when it was restored by Viollet-le-Duc, who worked at it for almost thirty years. It is the abode of the mausoleums of sovereigns and queens, and its roman-esque crypt houses the funeral monument of the Bourbon kings of France.

While the tentacular conurbation has overrun the basilica dedicated to the first bishop of Lutèce, in the west a wide wood-ed area still isolates it from the two illus-trious palaces in what is now called the "grande banlieue": Versailles and Saint-Germain-en-Laye.

A world of its own (a day will hardly do for a complete visit of the palace and the estate), Versailles tells the story of the reign of Louis XIV and of his successors, Louis XV and Louis XVI. The "house of kings", which was also that of princes, lords, and courtesans, is the symbol of the power and of the egocentricity of the Sun-King. This fabulous palace was once the capital of France, with the most important *Ministères* seated in the vicinity of the royal apartments. It was built by Le Vau and above all by Hardouin-Mansart, and decorated by Le Brun. Its endless façade faces the waterworks, the Grand Canal, and the immense gardens designed by Le Nôtre, a gardener of genius. Inside is a labyrinth of large and small apartments, drawing-rooms, corridors, stately or hidden stair-cases. The throngs of tourists who crowd there each year seem to have eyes only for the Galerie des Glaces, the perfect example of the splendour of the Grand Siècle, as well as for the bedrooms of the King and of the Queen, which have been restored

*Le Nôtre designed the gardens of Versailles, with pools and fountains set among trees, on the same grand scale as the palace itself (pre-ceding page). Later, Queen Marie-Antoinette played at being a she-pherdess in the "hamlet" of Trianon (above), which was built for her.*

with admirable care; but the palace also houses a refined opera-house by Gabriel, a very pretty chapel, and precious "cabinets". It was Louis-Philippe who, at the cost of a few mutilations, had the palace turned into a museum dedicated "To all the glories of France".

The museum-palace reigns over a vast estate divided into several parks. Its finer satellites are Grand Trianon and Petit Tria-

non. A mock hamlet was the last whim of Queen Marie-Antoinette, whom the mob had nicknamed "Madame Déficit" before taking her to the guillotine. Across from the iron railings of the palace stand the stables, "Grandes et Petites Écuries", at the edge of an unassuming city which, however, can boast of several fine hotels and of two interesting churches, Notre-Dame and the Saint-Louis cathedral.

Even though Versailles was his *magnum opus*, Louis XIV never completely forsook the palace of Saint-Germain, where he had been born and raised. Louis VI "le Gros", Saint-Louis, François I, and Henry IV had enlarged and embellished the old royal residence built at the edge of a forest which was full of game, and at the verge of a plateau overlooking the valley of the Seine. Louis XIV had five lodges built by

Whether it overlooks the "Green Carpet" or the Bassin d'Apollon (below), or is reflected in the water-beds studded with bronze allegories of France's main rivers, the Palace of Versailles attests the Sun-King's ambition to enhance his own reign by erecting a prestigious palace on a huge scale.

Hardouin-Mansart. However, the palace was partly ruined when Napoléon III decided to restore it in order to turn it into a museum of national antiquities; it then recovered the Renaissance aspect it had had under François I. Between Versailles and Saint-Germain, the palace of La Malmaison is not as grandiose in terms of architecture. However, it owes its celebrity to the memory of Napoléon I and of Joséphine, who both lived there. At the beginning of this century, it was made into an

*The Palace of Versailles is now a museum reflecting long periods of French history. Most of the court's celebrations were held in the Hall of Mirrors (above), which was desi-* *gned by Hardouin-Mansart and richly decorated by Le Brun. The memory of Louis XIV still lingers in the Small Apartments, particularly in the room where he died (left), and the Queen's* *room (opposite) looks today as it did in 1789, when Marie-Antoinette was driven away by the revolutionary mob.*

important museum dedicated to the memory of the imperial couple and of the glorious years of the Empire.

**The Heart of France.** The Paris conurbation, whose texture is looser at the periphery, has tentacles reaching to the surrounding cities, most of which have become dormitory-cities. It is located at the very centre of Île-de-France, a region which, along with Orléanais, was the original kingdom of France, and to which, one after the other, the provinces were to be added. Situated between Normandy and Champagne, the Bassin parisien is a region with a temperate climate and without sharp contrasts. It is a balance of forests and wheat and corn fields, of tree-clumps and vegetable-gardening, of plateaux and valleys. Paris is surrounded by factories, storehouses, and powerplants, mostly along the banks of the river Seine, both upstream and downstream. Industrial landscapes are offset by large tracts of untouched countryside strewn with manorhouses, châteaux, villages surrounded with country residences and old towns which have retained their character in spite of the all-encroaching capital. There are many noteworthy monuments in Île-de-France: in the southwest, the châteaux of Vaux-le-Vicomte and Fontainebleau; in the north and northeast, those of Écouen (now national museum of the Renaissance), of Chantilly, of Pierrefonds and of Compiègne, as well as the cathedrals of Senlis and Beauvais; in the southeast, Rambouillet and above all Chartres — two spires raised above an ocean of wheat.

Vaux-le-Vicomte bears witness to the inordinate pride of Superintendent Fouquet, a politician drunk with power. The gardens were a first hint of what was to become Versailles. The palace, built by Le Vau and decorated by Le Brun, astounded young Louis XIV, who soon became jealous of such splendour. The Sun being incapable of bearing the presence of other stars, the King hired the artists responsible for Vaux and prosecuted Fouquet, who ended his life in prison.

After another couple of bends, the Seine opens to one of the most beautiful forests of Île-de-France, named after Fontainebleau, a quiet little city in the midst of trees, and a luxurious palace in front of a park with ponds among which is "l'Étang de la Carpe", waterfalls, and the canal. The royal abode which Napoléon called "the house of centuries" is built around several courts in a rather loose way, which mirrors the successive phases of the construction. It all began as a manor-house for Louis VI "le Gros" and was later enlarged or remodelled by François I, Henry II, Henry IV, Louis XIII, Louis XIV and their successors. The palace, which is almost austere when seen from the outside, and to which access is given by a monumental staircase in the shape of a horseshoe, reveals a succession of large and small apartments, all extraordinarily luxurious. Three hours are hardly enough to visit the maze of galleries, drawing-rooms and bedrooms, the chapel, which was remodelled by Philibert Delorme, the museums, etc. The forest, with its sandy soil, its blocks of sandstone, and its steep cliffs where alpinists find

*Ile-de-France is a region strewn with palaces, some of which are*

an excellent training-ground, is astonishingly varied, dotted as it is with briar-patches. Most of the trees are oaks, beeches, birches and pines, spreading over almost a hundred square miles crossed with marked-out paths. The kings used to go hunting in the forest, and the pre-impressionist painters of the Barbizon school made it famous in the history of art.

**An historical suicide.** Two large churches watch over the northern part of Île-de-France. In Beauvais, only a miracle can account for the Saint-Pierre cathedral being saved from the bombardments of 1940. An unfinished Gothic masterpiece, it has no nave — only chancel and transept; both, however, are incredibly high. The quaint, quiet little city of Senlis harbours the old cathedral begun in 1153, now a composite edifice the towers of which the German artillery took aim at — in vain — in 1914. In the neighbourhood are remnants of a royal castle and of Gallo-Roman walls.

In Chantilly the lovely château is a jewel set in the middle of a forest and reflected in a mirror of water; it stands in large and beautiful gardens drawn by Le Nôtre, next to the hippodrome where the prize races of Diane and of the Jockey-Club are run every year. The XVIIIth century stables are superb. The Grand Condé made a point of embellishing the Renaissance building which had been admired by Charles Quint and by Henry IV. In 1671, he entertained the King and the whole court — 5,000 people, for whom sixty huge tables had been and remained set for three days in a row. When it turned out that he was short

*shown here: Fontainebleau (opposite), reflected in the Carps' Pond; Chantilly (top), which was remodelled in the XIXth century; Vaux-le-Vicomte (above), with its gardens designed by Le Nôtre.*

of roast meat and fish, Vatel, the head cook, committed suicide — thus making a name for himself in the gastronomic history of France. After being partly razed by the Revolution, the château was rebuilt by the Duke of Aumale; it now harbours a rich and eclectic museum with paintings from the XVIth to the XIXth centuries.

To the northeast of Chantilly, in the midst of the forest of Compiègne lies a clearing where, on November 11, 1918, the Allied Forces signed the Armistice with the Germans. Forests of full-grown oaks and beeches stand between Compiègne, an historical city on the banks of the Oise river, and the rocky spur upon which the castle of Pierrefonds stands. It is modelled after a typical feudal castle. However, the old fortress lay in ruin when Napoléon III asked Viollet-le-Duc to rebuild it. Com-

*With its two stone spires overlooking the wheat-covered Beauce plain, the cathedral of Chartres (preceding pages) symbolizes the spirit of faith which moved the builders, sculptors, and stained-glass window-makers of the Middle Ages. Here are shown the carved columns of the royal portal (above), a detail of the South porch (opposite), and Notre-Dame-de-la-Belle-Verrière (XIIIth century, right).*

piègne was a favourite hunting-place for all the kings of France, but Louis XIV found the old castle rather unconfortable: "In Versailles I live as a king, in Fontainebleau as a prince, in Compiègne as a peasant." As a consequence, the castle was enlarged to suit his taste. Louis XV, however, wished to do better still: he ordered Jacques and then Jacques-Ange Gabriel to rebuild a real palace, which was finished during the reign of Louis XVI. Napoléon III then fell in love with it, and he furnished the apartments anew. There, on a gray day, the emperor asked Mérimée to cheer up the court, upon which the writer wrote the well-known dictation with one hundred pitfalls; the empress made sixty mistakes! Nowadays, Compiègne harbours an interesting museum of carriages.

**The shrine in the wheat fields.** The highway runs in a straight line towards Chartres, turning just as one makes out the famous spires, the one romanesque, the other flamboyant. Chartres, a city with old, quaint streets, is the only important town in the unlimited horizon of Beauce, the granary of France, "cleaner than the cleanest sweep" (Péguy). Perceptible from a distance of twelve miles, the cathedral watches over an old district of steep, narrow streets. At once enormous and aerial, Notre-Dame is a fantastic poem in stone. Nobody knows who the architect was. After a fire destroyed the original church, very little of which is left, the present edifice was raised by the splendid effort of only one generation, which is the reason for its nearly perfect unity and for its incomparable purity.

The sculptor Auguste Rodin called it the acropolis of France because of its spiritual influence. The stately cathedral contains masterpieces of the romanesque such as

the royal portal and the old steeple, which do not in the least mar the unity of the ogival whole. The unusually wide nave is steeped in an extraordinarily bright blue light stemming from the unmatched windows of the XIIth and XIIIth centuries. The huge chancel is separated from the deambulatory by a wall with such a wealth of sculptures representing scenes from the Bible and the lives of Christ and the Virgin that it can truly be called a stone lacework. Adjoining the apse and a little above the level of the ground is the chapel of Saint-Piat housing the treasure of the cathedral, and under the latter is the largest crypt in France (it is 700 feet long and was built during the XIth century).

# *Orléanais*

*I*N THE HEART OF FRANCE, at the edge of Beauce and the Chartres country, the Orléanais was one of the very first additions to the crown of the Capet kings. It is a flat tract of land lying on both banks of a bend in the river Loire, and it is covered with the largest forest in France. On the south side of the river lies the austere Sologne, a huge hunting ground lit up by briar and gorse patches, and dotted with innumerable ponds.

In spite of its having been cruelly hit during World War II, Orléans has kept a

few old houses and a strange cathedral — an anachronism since it was built in the XVIIth and XVIIIth centuries in the Gothic style, and decorated with splendid woodworks.

The so-called house of Jeanne d'Arc was rebuilt after the Liberation of France in 1945 with old materials, as a token to the memory of the "Pucelle" who liberated the city from the English assailers in 1429. Ever since 1430, Jeanne has been the object of a celebration of processions and cavalcades every year on May 7 and 8.

# *Normandy*

REEN IS THE COLOUR of the *bocage*, of the broad meadows, and of the apple orchards: green is therefore the colour of Normandy, which consists in many different little regional units and many different kinds of land, all within the administrative limits of five *départements*: Seine-Maritime, Eure, Calvados, Manche and Orne. Rich grass and cattle herds are to be found almost everywhere, and apple-trees are often part of the landscape indeed. But in vain would one seek for a geographical unity in this region, which was modeled by history. Owing its name

to the fierce "men from the North" — Scandinavian pirates who settled and sobered down there after having terrorized Europe during the early Middle Ages, the former Dukedom of Normandy belongs both to the Armorican Mountains and to the Parisian Basin: layers of silica and white chalk are to be found in the east, hard granite rocks in the west.

Half-timbered, thatch-roofed houses are often considered as typical of Normandy; however, they only betoken certain parts of it, particularly the Auge valley. Elsewhere are to be found long farmhouses named

*courmasures* (Pays de Caux), or strong slate and granite houses (Cotentin), or yet still sober brick houses. This is why green, whether tender or aggressive, might well be the only common denominator — if it were not for rain, which is said to be unceasing even when it ceases.

Every Normandy-lover has a secret liking for the drizzle, the unpredictable downpours, and the showers that water the dust off the sky. The rain, which is fine, seldom cold, causes the slate roofs to glisten; it lashes at the beach-houses whenever the wind joins in; and everywhere it makes

*In Normandy, both the cities and the countryside bear the marks of the past. Shown here are the crowned tower of the Saint-Ouen church, built in the purest flamboyant Gothic style, and fine timber-framed houses in Rouen, the capital (left). Above is a typical Norman castle, in Saint-Germain-de-Livet, near Lisieux, with its large roofs, its stud work and its stone-and-brick checker-board pattern.*

32

green even greener. This is a country where a month's drought is a rarity. Which is no deterrent to the Deauville fans and to those familiar with the popular seaside resorts: "The only thing is to dress accordingly." A pair of boots and an oilskin coat are therefore necessary — but so are bathing suits. Even though the Channel, the ample tides of which cause the alternation of swimmers and shrimpers or pickers of seashells along its shores, may give the shivers to those who are unconditionally addicted to the Mediterranean sun, the healthy climate of Normandy is far from dreadful: it is as distant from scorching dog-days as it is from enduring frosts.

**The steeples of the martyred cities.** Normandy, being a country of middle-sized towns, of big, agricultural boroughs, and of

small villages drowned in green, has only four large cities, all of them victims of the war for being severely bombed during World War II. Le Havre, the second largest harbour in France, was almost completely remodelled after Auguste Perret's austerely geometric plans; Rouen, the museum-city, the admirable cathedral of which escaped the floods of fire only narrowly; Caen, where the old churches once kept watch over ruins; and Cherbourg, which was cruelly hit at the Liberation.

Rouen is generally considered as the capital of Normandy: it is the *préfecture* of Seine-Maritime, an important river harbour accessible to sea-going ships, and an industrial city which draws advantages from the relative vicinity of Paris. Held, lost, and held again by the English during the Middle Ages, the city where Jeanne d'Arc's pyre

was raised in 1431 nearly lost its superb Gothic cathedral, so well painted by Monet, as well as its courthouse, a masterpiece of the XVIth century, when it was crushed under the bombs during World War II. In spite of its now being surrounded by colourless modern suburbs, Rouen has retained a profound charm with its old centre spiked with steeples, its pedestrian streets, its lovely churches, and its Gros-Horloge, a Renaissance building flanked with a feudal belfry.

At once bold and lavish, displaying an extraordinary variety of Gothic styles, the cathedral is a towering beacon above the native town of Pierre Corneille, Fontenelle, and Gustave Flaubert. Restored after the war, it was not reopened for worship until 1956. The huge nave has kept its grandiose front, its famous, flamboyant Tour de Beurre, its Portail des Libraires — a unique, permanent display of medieval sculpture —, and its Portail de la Calende.

Inside, the tomb of the cardinals of Amboise, which was erected in the XVIth century in the Chapelle de la Vierge, is one of the gems of the Renaissance. In front of the cathedral, the picturesque Rue du Gros-Horloge looks like a scene set for an historical film with its cobblestones and its beautiful timbered houses. In the heart of old Rouen, it takes the tourist to the Place du Vieux-Marché, where Jeanne d'Arc was burnt alive.

Even more than Rouen, Caen, a river harbour connected to the sea by a nine-mile canal, suffered from the war: it was horribly mutilated by the uninterrupted bombardments of 1944. However, this industrial city with its well-known university was rebuilt with a certain harmony. The capital of Basse-Normandie, Caen, which is sometimes called the "Athens of Normandy," is so proud of its intellectual past that it has

*Tall slate-roofed houses, an old, quiet though colourful dock: such is Honfleur, which has lost nothing of its charm after being a retreat for many poets and artists of the XIXth century (above).*

*In Bayeux, one remembers William the Conqueror and his exploits. The famous tapestry (above), with its pictures of the Conquest of England, was made in Normandy upon the request of Odon de Conteville (right).*

seen to it that its castle was restored. A huge fortress built by William the Conqueror, which was the stronghold of the English when they ruled over the country, it now harbours two museums. As to the famous Abbaye aux Hommes and Abbaye aux Dames, and to the churches Saint-Étienne, Sainte-Anne, Saint-Julien, and Saint-Nicolas, it was a miracle if they escaped being ruined by the war, so that Caen is now a paradox in being a modern city watched over by old steeples. Caen also has connections with the rustic Pays d'Auge, the alluring home of camembert, cider, and calvados; with flat, rainy Bessin; and with the Norman *bocage* with its hedge-rimmed meadows. Nowhere is the coast very far, with its endless beaches of sand uncovered by the low tides, and its fishing and yachting harbours. On each summer Sunday, the inhabitants of Caen leave the city for the Côte de Nacre.

**The Normandy of cliffs and beaches.**
From Le Tréport to Mont-Saint-Michel, Normandy is wedded to the sea. To the east of Le Havre, the chalk plateau of Pays de Caux finds an abrupt end when its sheer white cliffs fall into the sea. A few miles from Fécamp, France's number one harbour for cod-fishing, the old resort of Étretat stretches its pebbled beach between two juttings of the chalk cliffs from which sticks out the celebrated Needle. The coast is cleft by the estuary of the Seine, which is spanned by the bold Tancarville bridge, high enough to let in the biggest cargoboats. The refineries and the industrial skyline of Le Havre are offset on the left bank by the old slate-roofed houses of the most picturesque harbour of Honfleur, a favourite resort for XIXth century painters and writers.

Deauville and Trouville, like twin sisters obstinately bent upon not being confused, are separated by the Touques, a tiny stream swollen by the sea-tides. Each of the two most famous resorts of the Côte Fleurie has its own casino and its *planches* — a wooden walk which runs along the edge of the sea where it is a rite to go for a stroll regardless of the weather. A rival of Cannes and Biarritz, easily accessible from Paris on a fast train or along a highway, Deauville is a seaside resort whose most faithful customers seem to have forgotten that it has a huge beach strewn with many colored tents the awnings of which are more often turned toward the walk than to the sea. With its luxurious villas and its bright casino, the resort, made fashionable by the Duke of Morny during the Second Empire and even more so by Eugène Cornuché after World War I, is a gathering place

*A region studded with churches and abbeys, Normandy has kept stately vestiges of the Romanesque period, such as the Benedictine abbey of Cerisy-la-Forêt, built by Robert le Magnifique and his son William the Conqueror (opposite).*

## Historical landmarks

In 911, King Charles the Simple officially gave the region to the Normans, Scandinavian pirates who had occupied it without official authorization. When the Duke of Normandy, William the Conqueror, became King of England, his duchy became an English fief from 1106 to 1204. Bitterly disputed over during the Hundred Years' War, Normandy fell once again under French rule in 1468. Europe's fate rested upon the Allied landing on Norman beaches on June 6, 1944. Already devastated by bombs, the region suffered enormously during the battles which lasted until september. Bayeux was the first French city to be liberated.

The chalk cliffs of Etretat, streak-
ed with silex, hollowed into natural
arches, and spiked with needles,
shelter the mild Pays de Caux, an area of meadows, groves, and
sparkling streams, from the storms of
the Channel.

for the smart set called "le Tout-Paris", and even for the international gotha; on weekends, however, it is literally weighted down by a more popular crowd who come from the less wealthy resorts of the vicinity in order to "have a look". The wealthier customers of Deauville seldom put out to sea; when they do, it is only in order to take their yacht out of a new, ill-matching harbour; they will also occasionally take a cautious swim in the superb, ultra-modern covered pool, or an aperitive stroll along the walk. Most of them are concerned only with the two leading activities in Deauville: racing and gambling. How many of them have ever gone to visit Lisieux, the hometown of Saint Thérèse, or the lovely Pays d'Auge nearby?

From the Seine estuary to the Cotentin, the seaside resorts are almost in a continuous line; they all have huge beaches when the tide is low. Some are more popular, like Blonville-Bénerville, Villers-sur-Mer, Riva-Bella, Luc-sur-Mer: others, with their large, wealthy villas, are more bourgeois. Cabourg is one of the latter, with the lingering memory of Marcel Proust, who stayed at the Grand Hotel, one of the very few "palaces" to be still standing along the coast of Normandy where, except for Deauville, the huge pleasure-domes of upperclass tourism have vanished — or been cut up into apartments.

In Ouistreham and Courseulles — the "oyster capital" of Normandy —, important yachting-harbours have been built, now all astir when the wind blows in the riggings of innumerable sailboats. Here, the latter outnumber motorboats by far. In Arromanches, in Omaha Beach, and in most of the resorts of the Côte de Nacre, people can still remember the most awesome event of World War II: the murderous landing of June 1944. The cemeteries with their endless rows of white crosses bear witness to the extreme violence of the fighting. In front of Arromanches, caissons are still sticking out of the sea, like stranded whales beaten by the waves. In the artificial harbour built by the Allied Forces, approximately 2,500,000 men and 500,000 vehicles were landed.

The three spires of the beautiful cathedral of Bayeux signal from afar the capital of Bessin. This old town possesses an incomparable treasure, the oldest series of captioned cartoons in the world: the "Telle du Conquest", also called Queen Mathilde's Tapestry — an immense embroidery made at the end of the XIth century, the fifty-eight

episodes of which narrate (sometimes with a good deal of humour) the epic of William the Conqueror, who took possession of England at the Battle of Hastings (1066).

Cotentin, a peninsula stretching its wooded patches and its valleys far out into the Channel, is a world of its own, with no spectacular resort, but which has an

endless charm (the little Vale of Saire is unique). Away from the coast one finds woods, enclosed fields, hollow paths, and panoramic heights; the shore is strewn with seaside resorts. Particularly enticing is the west coast with its huge beaches spiked with *bouchots* (wooden posts on which mussels grow) and its huge downs inter-

*Ever since the Middle Ages, the abbey of Mont-Saint-Michel (opposite), an immutable symbol of faith perched on top of a granite islet, has kept watch over one of the finest maritime sites in France.*

persed with spare tufts of grass. The Cape of Hague, still dreaded by sailors, has landscapes of a wild beauty.

In the centre of a large sandy bay, at the limit of Brittany, a prodigious solitary figure looms from afar: a pyramid of old houses surrounding an ancient abbey and squashed within ramparts, Mont-Saint-Michel sticks out a pointed spire bearing the statue of the Archangel. The Mont is not only a highly picturesque and beautiful place; it is an incomparable architectural curiosity. This fortress, much coveted by the English during the Hundred Years' War, is a wonder of the Middle Ages. It is still a goal for pilgrims and tourists. It is surrounded by sand and by salt meadows where sheep graze. The bay has gradually been drying up, so that the landscape is less beautiful with the sea now drawing away. The progression of the polders has been stopped, however; but important works will be needed before the bay can look again as it used to.

# Brittany

AT THE PROW OF EUROPE, a challenge to both the immense Atlantic ocean and the rolling waves of the Channel, the Breton peninsula, with its jagged shores, is an example of unity in diversity. It is a many-sided region, and yet it retains a specific character. Highly independent and profoundly original, it has never quite melted into the national pot. "We hereby perpetually join the Dukedom of Brittany with the Kingdom of France, that they can never be separated...", François I declared in the Edict of Union; however, four centuries later, the Breton people are still jealous of their idiosyncracies and of their old celtic language, which is still very much alive although it is not spoken everywhere: after being banned by schoolmasters, it is now being taught in universities, and it inspires the bards who use today's rhythms in their lyrics on eternal Brittany.

In the country of mysterious megaliths — dolmens or menhirs raised much before the Celtic invasion —, the people remember their druids and their saints, their dukes (particularly the Duchess Anne, who married two Kings of France and had them vow to respect the freedom of her homeland), and their "chouans" who rebelled against the out-and-out centralisation enforced by the Revolution. After having been forsaken during the great upheavals of the XIXth century, being relatively poor and feeling bitter over seeing its younger people emigrate, Brittany is now undergoing a major change. Its people are willing to open up its beaches, its churches and its calvaries decorated with scenes from the Scriptures, but they just will not let their country be turned into a reserve for tourists. The times of Bécassine are over. With occasional fits of anger, the Bretons now demand that their economy be developed as in the rest of France, and they will see to it that their personality be respected.

Whether stupidly caricatured or praised with high-flown lyricism, Brittany is no topic for ready-made formulas. Its human specimens are more varied than one would think; the four major Breton dialects coexists with forms of *patois* derived from the French; and *Armor* (the coast) seems quite different from *Arcoat* (the interior). With its mild winters, its precocious springs, and its warm summers, Brittany has specific colours and yet it can be divided into many local units. "A hundred parishes, a hundred churches", says a proverb expressing the diversity of the great peninsula. With a population of 3.2 millions, Brittany officially consists of five *départements*: Finistère, Côtes-du-Nord, Ille-et-Vilaine, Morbihan and Loire-Atlantique; but the Vannes region, the "Pays Bigouden," Trégor, Léon and Brière and many other "islands" have managed to keep their originality. There are as many Brittanies as there are kinds of head-dresses.

**Arcoat with its heaths and woods.** The green and golden country of heaths and woods includes hills, plateaux, and meadows hemmed in by hedges and glens. Strewn with ponds and châteaux, crossed by hollow paths, the Paimpont forest is haunted by the legendary heroes of Brittany, the Knights of the Round Table, Vivien and Merlin the Enchanter. Near where the new, automobile-driven "druids" meet is the huge military camp of Coëtquidan-Saint-Cyr.

The forest, which is not in a very good state although it has been reafforested, stops only a dozen miles away from Rennes, the capital of Brittany, a former medieval city almost totally destroyed by fire in 1720. An intellectual, academic, and administrative centre, it can boast of some fine classical buildings such as the Place du Palais and the old Parliament, of a baroque townhall, and of a few very old houses as well as of the remarkable Museum of Brittany (the best visual introduction to the many aspects of the province), and of a rich museum (paintings, china).

Arcoat also consists in the heaths of Ménez-Hom and Lanvaux, the lake of Guerlédan and the gorges of the Blavet, the Black Moutains, the lonely, rocky Monts d'Arrée strewn with yellow patches of gorse, broom, and colza. The Arrée region, with its massive dark shale houses, often steeped in fog, is particularly rainy: a barrier between Léon and Cornouaille, it raises its

*Out of their rough, granite-ridden ground, the people of Brittany have hewn churches and calvaries in keeping with their mysticism. One of the most original of these monuments is the "parish enclosure" of Guimiliau, with a calvary of two hundred sculpted characters (left). Cities and walls are also made from granite: for example, Saint-Malo (above), which was made famous by its corsairs.*

melancholy hills in front of the Atlantic, and stops the clouds. The regional natural park of Armorique includes the Monts d'Arrée, the mouth of the Aulne, the Crozon peninsula as well as Ouessant, an island with a formidable crown of reefs.

**A coast with a thousand indentations.**
The beautiful coastline of Brittany, a prey to both winds and waves, is cut up into narrow *rias* and wide estuaries into which tidal currents flow in and out; it opens into bays, gulfs, and innumerable coves well-protected from the wind. Studded with seaside resorts as well as with modest holiday places, with tiny beaching harbours

and with big fishing harbours crowded with colourful trawlers, it unwinds its jagged contours from the purlieus of Mont-Saint-Michel to the mouth of the Loire.

At the north-eastern corner of Brittany, watch is kept by the city of Saint-Malo, closed in its walls and rebuilt after the bombardments of 1944. The city boasts of its famous Quiquengrogne tower, its dungeon, its restored cathedral, but also of its corsairs, and of Jacques Cartier, Duguay-Trouin, Surcouf, Chateaubriand (who was buried on the Grand-Bé islet) and Lammenais. Saint-Malo and the two neighbouring cities of Saint-Servan and Paramé have now been wedded into one township. In

the latter, during the equinox tides, the sea lashes at the long sea-wall.

The mouth of the Rance river separates Saint-Malo from Dinard, the largest resort on the Côte d'Émeraude. A short cut from

*In Finistère (literally the end of the earth), Brittany cleaves the ocean with its rocky, jagged headlands. Above is shown the double head of Cape Sizun: the Pointe du Van with the Saint-They chapel, and, looming in the mist, the foam-fringed Pointe du Raz. This is the heart of Breton-speaking Brittany, where traditions are kept, including lacework and old headdresses (opposite are shown headdresses from Plougastel).*

one to the other is now provided by the road on top of the electric power plant, but it is preferable to drive around the deep gash of the river in order to see Dinan, a picturesque and very interesting fortified mediev-

al city. Built upon a table of rocks looking over the opening of the estuary and defended by an enormous dungeon, the city still shows streets of another age, a belfry with a clock as old as 1498, the flamboyant

### Historical landmarks

*Britanny, a region riddled with neolithic menhirs and dolmens, was settled by the Celts during the VIth century B.C. They called the area Armor (the Sea country). Starting in 56 B.C., the area fell under Roman influence. Breton groups migrated to Armorique around 460 A.D. from Great Britain. This trans-Channel immigration continued for two centuries. In 799, Charlemagne took over Brittany, and appointed Nominoë, a count from Vannes, as its duke. He soon freed himself from Franc rule. In the middle of the IXth century, Brittany became a practically independent principality. Duke François II (1458-1488) allied himself with Louis XI's enemies. His daughter, Anne de Bretagne, married Charles VIII, then his successor, Louis XII, but remained the ruler of a duchy whose independence she assured. Her daughter, Claude de France, married François I, who published the Union edict in 1532. Brittany then became a French province. During the Revolution, Breton royalists called chouans caused Southern Brittany to rebel.*

42

Saint-Malo church and an unfinished basilica on the walls of which can be seen the
successive architectural styles developed
between the XIIth and the XVIth centuries.

The old town of Saint-Brieuc, set
between two hills a few miles from the sea,
is watched over by a fortified cathedral of
the XIIth and XIIIth centuries. Formerly the
harbour of fishermen who would sail to
Iceland for long campaigns on fine schoo-
ners, Paimpol now nestles in a nook
along the coast, between the Arcouest point
and Bréhat, a flowery island forbidden to
cars. In Perros-Guirec, a resort in northern
Brittany, the jagged granite is pink, and all
ablaze when the sun sets. Between the
huge blocks shaped like fantastic creatures
and the ruined castles are to be found tiny
harbours, small beaches, and family residences. Next to the Trégor country is the
Léon country, with Saint-Pol and its old
houses clustered about the cathedral; Ros-
coff, with its Renaissance steeple and its
harbours. The mild weather and the rich

soil favour the exportation of fresh vegetables such as potatoes, onions, and cauli-
flowers. The Isle of Batz, anchored a few
miles away from the coast, seems to screen
in the harbour of the car-ferries plying to
Plymouth.

West of the Aber-Wrac'h — the estuary
of the Witch — with its uniquely beautiful
landscapes, the chaotic coast folds back in
front of the ocean: here is Finistère, the
wind-swept "land's end" of innumerable
legends. Off its coast is Ouessant, the
"isle of dread" often drowned in the mists
of the Iroise sea — a bastion of granite and
shale hemmed in by deadly reefs: "Qui voit
Ouessant voit son sang" (Whoever sees
Ouessant sees his own blood). Two thousand islanders still live on this now barren
rock, raising small black-and-white sheep
and gathering sea-weed. South of the large
indentation in the coast line, the isle of
Sein is less grandiose but no less desolate
than Ouessant. On several occasions, it
was nearly submerged by the Atlantic. It

*Brittany, a region steeped in mystery, has retained its legends. The druids may have disappeared from the sanctuaries, but in Carnac the menhirs are still to be seen in their awesome alignments (above). Frightening stories of roving wraiths and of boats manned with dead people hover over the Raz de Sein, riddled with reefs and run though by headlong currents. "Whoever sees Sein sees his own end", the saying went. Modern seamen no longer fear the island (right page), which nonetheless remains a mysterious granite slab worn by winds and seas.*

44

is still peopled with fishermen who venture away among the reefs and the currents. Between the Pointe du Raz and the Pointe du Van, a wild, barren cove in Cape Sizun has been called "la Baie des Trépassés".

**The naval base and the drowned city.** Before becoming a large modern city with broad avenues and flower gardens, Brest was pitilessly battered by the allied air forces aiming at the naval base. The city overlooks a roadstead with a narrow channel somewhat like an inner sea in which the French Navy have established both a naval base and a naval dockyard. Apparently beaconing to Brest from its location south of the Crozon peninsula, Douarnenez, formerly the capital of Cornouaille, now the sixth fishing harbour in France, lies at the far end of a bay into which, after the legend, the ancient town of Ys was drowned through the fault of a disobedient princess.

Now the capital of Cornouaille, Quimper, which is beaconed by the steeples of a cathedral under construction during several centuries, is an old town built in granite on the Odet, a river running down from the Black Mountains into a fjord-like estuary. Quimper is the starting-point of many trips in South Finistère, to Pont-l'Abbé, to Bénodet, to the walled city of Concarneau and its harbour with its blue nets, to Pont-Aven where the memories of Gauguin and of Théodore Botrel the *chansonnier* still linger. Lorient (formerly "l'Orient") used to be the seat of the Compagnie des Indes. After World War II, it was rebuilt into a clean, geometric but cold-looking, functional modern city, whose fishing harbour is the second in France. Quite different is Sainte-Anne-d'Auray, an inland small town which every year in July is the seat of the biggest *pardon* (a processional pilgrimage) in Brittany: it is the Breton version of Lourdes, with a basilica full of innumerable ex-votos.

**From the menhirs to the châteaux of the Dukes of Brittany.** Rows after rows of menhirs, dolmens, and barrows — the awe-inspiring megaliths can only make one dream and build hypotheses, as no one so far has been able to solve the mystery of Carnac. Nearby are to be found Carnac-Plage, a family holiday resort, and the big yachting-harbour of La Trinité-sur-Mer.

Once an island, the narrow peninsula of Quiberon has partially retained its wild aspect with the waves breaking upon its shores. Now welded to the continent, it is often crowded in summertime, with traffic jams on every sunny weekend. Quiberon has a well-known centre for salt-water cures, and an old sardine-fishing harbour, where one can sail for Belle-Île, a large island with an indented coast, tiny beaches, and varied landscapes. Le Palais, the small capital of the island, is a former stronghold overlooked by a picturesque citadel; on the Côte sauvage is hidden one of the natural wonders of Brittany, the huge grotto of l'Apothicairerie.

Vannes is an old, peaceful, and picturesque city, whose people are proud of their cathedral and of their big-bellied houses; it squats at the far end of a deep gulf in which are sheltered about sixty islets as well as the enchanted garden of Île-aux-Moines. At the entrance of the "Little Sea" of Morbihan, a stretch of shallow water in a mild country where laurels, myrtles, camelias and fig-trees grow, Locmariaquer and Port-Navalo keep watch. Vannes is a good place from which to take short trips inland, to Ploërmel, one of the oldest cities in the dukedom; to Josselin and its castle; to Redon and the church of Saint-Sauveur, the quays along the Vilaine, and the canal; and to Pontivy, an old Arcoat city whose gabled houses nestle under a big feudal castle.

The large harbour of Saint-Nazaire is not far from either the marshes of Grande Brière with their shivering reed-beds, or Guérande, a jewel of feudal architecture at the edge of the salt-marshes. Although there is nothing Breton about it, La Baule has one of the finest and safest sand-beaches in France. Brittany merges into the Loire valley in the very heart of the muscadet region, at Nantes, a large, growing city and a sea-harbour on the banks of the river (the port authority also controls Saint-Nazaire, Donges, Paimbœuf, etc.). Enclosed in the chess-board pattern of a modern suburbia, Nantes has kept a castle, surrounded by ramparts and moats, which used to be the residence of the Dukes of Brittany (now a museum), an austere cathedral, venerable houses, and beautiful hotels; however, the harmonious though severe Place Royale had to be rebuilt in part after the havoc played by World War II.

# *Maine*

**B**ETWEEN THE LOIRE and Normandy, not far from the vistas opened by Perche, Le Mans lies at the crossroads of the main itineraries of western France: between Tours and Alençon (a fine city in Normandy, well-known for its lace-work), halfway between Chartres and Rennes. The former capital of Maine County, now the meeting-place of automobile fans with its twenty-four hours' mad race, Le Mans was heavily bombarded between 1940 and 1944; fortunately, however, its splendid cathedral and the old district with its Gallo-Roman walls were saved.

*After it became a duchy in the Xth century, and as it was intent upon preserving its independence, Brittany fortified itself with citadels and fortresses. At the end of the Middle Ages, however, the castles were replaced by peaceful manorhouses such as the Château des Rochers, near Vitré, where the Marquess of Sévigné came to rest, notwith standing her letter-writing activity.*

# *Anjou*

A STATELY WATER AVENUE for the boatmen of yore, the winding Loire maps out the route of the châteaux. Its incomparable "Val" began as the garden of the great feudal princes, only to become the capital of France when the wandering kings took to moving from one château to another with their crew of courtesans, counsellors and mistresses in motley caravans loaded with chests, silverware, and tapestries... The river, which is often

bloodless and lazy, though sometimes angry, seems at first to be drawn toward Île-de-France, only to turn south-west at Orléans, after which it directs its winding course to the Atlantic. Once called "the Kings' boulevard and a gallery of masterpieces", the changing Loire mirrors the moving sky as it flows across harmonious landscapes through which unhurried tributaries flow slantwise. In times of low water, the river seems to be looking for its way in a bed too big for it; it hems in innumerable islands and sand-shoals; sometimes, it seems to lose itself in dead-ends. However, one should never trust the Sleeping Beauty: its laziness is full of guile; in times of flood, its flow can hardly be contained by the big earth-banks along which the roads run parallel.

The river bestows a certain unity upon the valley, which is characterized by moderation — anything but spectacular contrasts. Toward its end is Anjou, south of Brittany and Maine, a great historical region as it was the homeland of the Plantagenets, who wore the English crown, and of the "good" King René, who was Duke of Bar and Lorraine as well as Count of Provence and potential ruler of the Kingdom of Naples. The former dukedom, with its blurred borders and its varied landscapes — forests,

meadows, and tree-nurseries — gets its colours from its many flower-beds and its wines from Savennières, Layon, Saumur. It is studded with châteaux and manor-houses (le Plessis-Macé, le Plessis-Bourré, Montgeoffroy, Brissac) as well as with beautiful villages built in bright stones.

Angers, the capital, spreads over a hill on the bank of the river Maine. Its modern periphery encloses a highly interesting historical nucleus, with the Gothic cathedral, the picturesque Adam house, the Barrault Museum, and the Saint-Aubin tower. The castle was proudly built during the XIIIth century in front of the river; it looks like a formidable fortress with dark walls striped with white, and with its decapitated towers. Behind these forbearing walls are to be found elegant buildings of the XVth century as well as the modern Grande Galerie, which houses the extraordinary, bright-coloured XVIth century tapestry called *L'Apocalypse,* a gift of King René. After being set aside and partly mangled, it was restored as the original red and blue puzzle illustrating various episodes of Saint John's *Revelation.*

East of Anjou, in a vine-growing country of cliffs tapped with galleries used as wine stores and mushroom beds, Saumur

*Angers, a city hugging the banks of the Maine river, has preserved many tokens of its rich history. Among them the feudal castle stands out with its walls spiked with towers (above). Many houses also represent the past of the capital — such as the Adam house, with its sculpted facade, of which a detail is shown above. In the Anjou region, Saumur (right page) is proud of its castle. Here, however, the Loire river can be seen leisurely winding its way among islands and sand shoals.*

spreads out below an elegant XIVth century castle still very much like its miniature representation in the *Très Riches Heures du Duc de Berry*. In it are to be found a Museum of Decorative Arts and a museum devoted to horses: this is because, even before the Revolution, Saumur became the home of a riding school which in 1814 was turned into the famous *Cadre noir*. The church of Notre-Dame-de-Nantilly is the oldest in the city, but more picturesque is Notre-Dame-des-Ardilliers, which is fronted with a quaint rotunda topped with a dome with lantern-lights.

In the vicinity of Saumur, at the crossroads of Touraine, Anjou, and Poitou, is the Abbey of Fontevrault, which was founded at the end of the XIth century or in the very first years of the XIIth. It benefitted from the favours of the Plantagenêts, who are buried there, and it became a religious centre for both sexes, with an abbess from the nobility holding sway over monks as well as nuns.

### Historical landmarks

*Anjou belonged to a line of hereditary counts, the Foulques. One of them, Geoffroi, liked to wear a genista branch in his hat, which is why the family name "Plantagenêt" became that of his line. He married an English princess named Mathilde. Their son, Henri Plantagenêt, became king of England after marrying Eleanor of Aquitaine (whose dowry gave him all of south-west France). Philippe Auguste seized Anjou in 1205 and, with Maine, the province was handed over to Charles, Louis VIII's son. Charles founded the second house of Anjou, which was succeeded by the dynasty of Good King René, an artist and patron of the arts. Anjou came once again under French rule at the end of the XVth century, after the prince's death.*

*The homeland of the Plantagenêts has kept its patrimony: thus, the castle of Angers harbours an unrivaled collection of tapestries, the most famous of which is the Apocalypse (XIVth century, above), and the abbey of Fontevrault (opposite), which was long used as a prison, has recovered its original appearance.*

# *Touraine*

CALLED THE "GARDEN OF FRANCE" or the "gentle country", Touraine, with its large forests and its charming countryside, lies on both sides of the Loire, fighting with Anjou over Bourgueil, merging into the Blois region, and drifting into Berry along the rivers Indre and Cher. It is a flowery country, where white houses as well as cave-dwellings are dressed with rosetrees and wistarias, and it is rich with outstanding towns and villages, famous castles, and innumerable manor-houses.

Tours, set as it is between the Loir and the Cher and in control of an important crossroads, was not left undamaged after World War II. However, the capital of Touraine — a middle-class city enlivened by a student population and peaceful without being boring — has kept its cathedral (XIII-XIVth centuries) and boldly renovated the old, picturesque district with street names evocative of the Middle Ages. It also owns fine museums, and it is the starting-point for a number of musts: trips to the wonderful castles of Chinon, where you would expect to meet with the Pucelle or with Rabelais' heroes; to Loches, a medieval city with a triple wall; and to Amboise.

**Stones jewels.** Between Tours and Chinon, whose ruined castle is brushed by long-famous vineyards, Azay-le-Rideau looms into sight amid a grove of trees: this slender, dazzling masterpiece of the Renaissance in Touraine, washed by the river

Indre, was compared by Balzac to a many-faceted diamond. Nearby, Villandry raises its proud profile in front of the geometric lace-work of its extraordinary gardens, which have been patiently restored to their XVIth century state. On the other bank of the Loire, the stern-looking castle of Langeais was refurnished and its walls hung with splendid tapestries, so that it again looks as it did when Anne de Bretagne married Charles VIII in front of the stately mantelpiece of the large drawing-room.

The lazy, winding stream of the Berry-born Cher flows under the six arches of the castle of Chenonceau, the gracefully aristocratic object of the love of Diane de Poitiers, Henry II's favourite mistress, who asked Philibert Delorme, the renowned architect, to enlarge the luxurious residence given her by her royal lover.

Here are Vouvray and Montlouis, whose white wine vineyards echo each other across the river, then Amboise — an old city with a sweet name, crouching under a palace-like

**storical landmarks**

*ter being briefly incorporated by England, uraine suffered from many a strife before ing definitively returned to France in 59. From Saint Louis to François I, most of e kings of France lived in Touraine and in Blois region, at least for a time. As he grew , Louis XI even came to live in the châu of Plessis-lès-Tours. The bridge-cities of Loire valley suffered great damage during rld War II.*

*In Blois (the entrance door of the château is shown above), the flamboyant Gothic style reflecting the Italian influence can be seen in the stone festoons, the reliefs, the arabesque lines, and the openwork sculptures.*

*In the châteaux region, here is Azay-le-Rideau (opposite), a pure jewel set on the Indre river, which mirrors a harmonious design typical of Renaissance refinement.*

52 castle, which is equally majestic and elegant. With a Gothic chapel chiseled like a jewel, it was one of the first abodes of the kings of France. In the nearby manor-house of Clos-Lucé still lingers the memory of a genius: François I made a gift of it to Leonardo da Vinci, who thought of controling the Loire with dams, and may have had a hand in the building of Chambord, the highlight of the Blois region. On the road from Amboise to Blois is to be found a fancy fortress, Chaumont, which Catherine de Médicis, after she became the widow of

Henry II, forced her rival Diane de Poitiers (upon whom she had long waited to wreak her revenge) to take in exchange of dearer Chenonceau.

**Two spectacular sights: Blois and Chambord.** The composite castle of Blois can tell historical and architectural tales dating back a long time: in the form of an incomplete rectangle surrounding a XIIIth century state room, it was built little by little. Only in the XVIIth century did François Mansart build the Gaston d'Orléans

wing. The assassination of the Duke of Guise, ordered by Henry III, was performed there after the all-powerful leader of the Ligue had pitted his forces against the Crown. "You have cut well, my son; now you must sew", the Queen is reported to have muttered after hearing about the murder. The arrangement of Blois into whimsical tiers pleased Victor Hugo. After World War II, restoration was carried on intelligently within the city of Blois, whose irregular lay-out was kept, and where rebuilding was harmoniously made to match the

old *hotels,* the abbey, and the cathedral of Saint-Louis. The ogival bridge built in the xVIIth century over the Loire by Jacques Gabriel is an invitation to visit the haughty, classical Cheverny with its splendid furniture, and to discover Chambord.

The largest of the Loire valley châteaux is set in the middle of a huge, fenced-in estate peopled by oars, does, and deer; it is a welter of arabesques, terraces, turrets, gables, pinnacles, and carved mantel-pieces. The first stone of this admirably odd edifice was laid in 1519. Chateau-briand compared it to "a woman whose hair has been blown straight up", and Victor Hugo described it as "a place of fairies and knights". In spite of its being set squat on the ground, it looks like a challenge to gravity. It can boast of odd inventories: 440 rooms, a large double-wound stair-case, 84 lesser flights of stairs, dozens of pinnacles, mantel-pieces, and column-capitals. Chambord was the scene of François I's reception of Charles Quint; and there it was that Louis XIV called Lully and Molière and his company for the first performance of *Le Bourgeois Gentilhomme.*

Along with such other castles as Beauregard (with a remarkable portrait gallery), Villesavin and Herbault, Chambord stands in a wooded region which is part of Sologne,

*Chenonceaux, surrounded by gardens and woods, is a fine palace built during the Renaissance in the very bed of the Cher river, on the piers of a former mill.*

*According to Victor Hugo, Chambord is the symbol of "all magic, all poetry, all folly". It can also be described as "a palace for knights and fairies" (following pages).*

53

a huge hunting ground dotted with many
ponds. Several other castles are to be
found on the right bank of the Loire in the
part of Blésois which gradually merges into
Dunnois and Orléanais: the hall of Ménars,
remodelled by Madame de Pompadour, was
enlarged by Gabriel, a personal friend
of hers, and completed by Soufflot. The
severe-looking Talcy was rebuilt at the
beginning of the XVIth century by Ber-
nard Salviati, a businessman from Florence
whose female descendants twice played a
part in the history of French literature, as
Ronsard fell in love with his daughter
Cassandra, and Agrippa d'Aubigné with
his granddaughter Diane. From Talcy to
Mer the road to be taken, called the road of
roses, is well-named as it is made fragrant
with some ten thousand rose bushes.

Beaugency, which was one of the cities
delivered from English rule by Jeanne d'Arc
during her campaign of 1429, has kept its
old houses, its stone bridges, its ancient
abbey, and the César tower which inspired
Victor Hugo for one of the settings of his
play *Marion Delorme*. The castle, built by
Dunois, one of the Pucelle's comrades,
harbours a regional museum of popular
arts and crafts.

Away from the river, in the north of
Blésois, the "gentle Loir", as Ronsard called it, is to be found lingering in Vendôme,
whose mixed-style minster displays the
white stone lace-work of a flamboyant front
beside a strong, medieval steeple.

# Berry

AS GEORGE SAND described it so
well, Berry is a country of fruitful
plains, wooded areas, and modest
valleys, dotted with lovely Romanesque
churches and châteaux, the richest of
which is Talleyrand's at Valençay. Bourges, which was the capital of France during
the reign of Charles VII, is a great city for
art. Towering above the city is the stately
mass of the cathedral, a masterpiece of the
XIIIth century with its five naves and its five
carved portals, a chancel with five adjoining
chapels, a double deambulatory, and admirable painted-glass windows with medal-
lions. One of the finest medieval houses
in the whole of France is the Gothic residence of financier Jacques Cœur. The gardens of the Archbishopric are believed to
be by Le Nôtre. The private mansions
built in the Renaissance style vie with each
other for elegance, and there are many old
houses with overhanging upper storeys.

*The Saint-Étienne cathedral in
Bourges is undoubtedly one of the
finest examples of Gothic architecture (see following pages).*

*The Val de Loire
is still haunted
by the memory
of François I,
who gave
it many
of its jewels.
Here is shown
one of the balconies
of the François I
staircase in Blois.*

# Poitou and Charentes

THE LANGUAGES OF OÏL AND OC as well as the north and the south are blended rather than confronted in the region of Poitou and Charentes, a border land where the foolhardy Arab conquest was stopped in 732, where English and French troops fought each other, and where pilgrims passed on their way to Compostelle. South-east of the secretive province of Vendée, a region of woods and canals the shoreline of which rounds out south of the island of Noirmoutier, the threshold of the South-West is a flat countryside stretching east toward Limousin, and south-east toward Périgord. Poitiers, the historical capital of Poitou, which is also an important art centre, must share its influence with Angoulême, the head of an old dukedom, and with La Rochelle, a fortified harbour which was once the key to Aunis, an old province overlapping two *départements:* Charente-Maritime and Deux-Sèvres.

In Poitiers, where the steep streets cling to the hillside, the Saint-Pierre cathedral combines the Romanesque and the "Angevin" Gothic styles, whereas Notre-Dame-la-Grande, with its XIIth century front, is a pure example of Romanesque art. The city, which was made famous by its university as early as the XVth century, can also boast of other fine churches, of the remains of its old ducal palace, of its old houses and of

### Historical landmarks

*Caesar's legions held Aquitania (the Water country) when it was inhabited by various Gaulois peoples, and the South-West has kept many vestiges of the prosperous gallo-roman period. Aquitaine was attached to the Franc kingdom when it was owned by Louis le Pieux, one of Charlemagne's sons; it then became a duchy, and in 1152 it was incorporated in England when the duchess Eleanor, who had been repudiated by the king of France, married Henry II Plantagenêt, a prince from Anjou who was the heir to the English throne. Aquitaine — or Guyenne — was larger than what it is today, as it included Poitou, Limousin, Périgord, Agenois, Gascogne and part of Saintonge. Bitterly fought over by England and France, it became permanently French after the battle of Castillon (1453). Thirty years earlier, Poitou, after being reconquered by du Guesclin and given to the Duke of Berry, was attached to France.*

*Poitou, a region with a mild climate and many shades in a landscape uniting the North to the South of France, reveals its character as much through the variety of scenery (left is shown the Marais, one of the most surprising settings in Poitou, with its streams [conches] covered with duckweed and the traditional black boats of the maraîchins), as well as through the innumerable shrines left by the Middle Ages. This is because Poitou, an important stop on the way to Saint-Jacques-de-Compostelle, has preserved many tokens of the time when it was one of the most active centres of romanesque architecture. The poitevin style is best seen in the elaborate facade of the former collegiate church of Notre-Dame-la-Grande in Poitiers (right page). It is a highly decorative style, as shown in the sculptured capitals of Saint-Pierre-de-Chauvigny (opposite), which were unfortunately painted over in the XIXth century.*

the gardens of Blossac, a panoramic terrace laid by an intendant in the XVIIth century. In Angoulême, a city also built upon a hill, the finest prospects are offered by a walk on the ramparts. The cathedral, which is mostly from the XIIth century, displays an extraordinary collection of medieval statues on its highly elaborate front. La Rochelle was once an independent harbour, which was later fortified by Vauban; it is the most interesting city on the coast, with its tidal dock guarded by two towers, its lively wharves, its high Lanterne tower, its XVIth century townhall, and its charming Rue des Merciers. With the addition of La Pallice, a deep-water harbour for the bigger ships, La Rochelle can harbour hundreds of trawlers and other boats; tons of fish are auctioned there, and are dispatched throughout France.

Like a long raft moored to La Pallice, the low isle of Ré stretches at water level between the "Pertuis breton" and the "Pertuis d'Antioche". In spite of the summer invasion of tourists marvelling at the Ré women's traditional bonnet called *quichenotte* (kiss-me-not), the island retains some character with its light-houses, its salt-works, its oyster-beds, and the incredibly narrow lanes of Ars-en-Ré. The second largest French island after Corsica, Oléron extends Saintonge under an often cloudy sky. The islanders grow early vegetables and a rather ordinary wine; but mostly they live on oyster-breeding. They also have an original way of fishing, by trapping the fish into closed ponds and letting the water flow out through railings at low tide.

Les Sables-d'Olonne is the big seaside resort in the south of Vendée, not far from the fish-preserves; its long Remblai stretches along a fine beach, from the gates of the harbour to the Corniche and on to the Puits d'Enfer. Facing the Pointe de Grave, Royan controls the Gironde estuary. Having lost its old rococo hotels, its large villas and its casino under the heavy bombardments of 1944, it remains an important holiday resort, but its long beach is now hemmed in by concrete. The fine church built in the 1950's may impress one by its slenderness, but the pink tiles of the roofs cannot really warm up this modern, spacious city.

Charente is the home of oysters and cognac. The latter, locally called "cougna", is the product of the distillation of white wines. The brandy, which has been famous throughout the world for two centuries, owes its savour and aroma to its being

aged in casks made of Limousin oak. The three stars (supposedly invented by Hennessy in the XVIIIth century) mean that the brandy is at least one and a half year old; the letters V.S.O.P. (Very Superior Old Pale) mean that it is over four years old. The town of Cognac is surrounded by the vineyards of Grande Champagne, Petite Champagne, and Borderies, although in fact the vineyards extend much farther, to the two Charente *départements,* as far as Saintes, a lovely city with fine churches, medieval façades and elaborate ironwork.

*In La Rochelle (opposite),* ever since the wars of the Middle Ages, two towers have kept watch over the entrance of a now peaceful harbour. On the island of Noirmoutier, the castle overlooks the coast of Vendée (below).

# Aquitaine

**A**N OLD PROVINCE which, under the name of Guienne, was an English possession for three centuries, Aquitaine once included Poitou, Limousin, Berry, Auvergne and Saintonge. It was returned to the Crown of France after the Hundred Years' War, made larger by the annexation of the once independent Béarn. The capital of this vast region is Bordeaux, a wealthy city built in dazzling white stone.

With nearly 600,000 inhabitants if one includes the suburbs, Bordeaux is the largest city in the South-West, a regional metropolis to "balance" the influence of Paris. However, Bordeaux is also — a fact which is not universally known — one of the finest cities in France. While in the 1970's the ambitious, ultra-contemporary districts of Mériadec and Lac came forth under the din of the concrete-mixers, resurfacing and renovating gave a new life to the incomparable set of buildings designed by the royal intendants in the XVIIIth century. The scraping process uncovered hundreds of mascarons (grotesque masks) that had been encrusted by time, while housefronts were restored to their original warm colour, a light, luminous fawn against which stand out the wonderful balconies painted anew in a deep blue. The old harbour with curved wharves called "port de la lune" throve in Gallo-Roman times, easily adapted itself to the English rule (under which the wine trade was promoted), and managed to keep its privileges even when it went back to the crown of France — rather unwillingly. Such an active city was cramped within its ramparts, a medieval carcan which was got rid of shortly before the Revolution, at the same time as many Roman vestiges as well as medieval monuments were razed.

Bordeaux owes a lot to Victor Louis, the architect of the Grand Théâtre, and to Prince-Archbishop Ferdinand Maximilien Mériadec de Rohan, who built the palace which is now the town-hall. The city owes even more to the intendants of both Louis XV and Louis XVI. While holding the city under strict control, they opened it on the Garonne, planned its "Grande Façade" along the river as well as the avenues, the admirable Stock Exchange building, and harmonious squares. The city-councillors often complained that the budget was being overstepped, but the ambit-

*The Place de la Bourse in Bordeaux, such as it was designed in the XVIIIth century by intendants, with elegant townhouses with sculptured façades and bell-towers, and large squares brightened up by bubbling fountains.*

ious representatives of the king did lay down the sumptuous city-planning which is still there. Only the area between the church of Saint-Pierre and the church of Saint-Michel has kept its medieval confusion behind the elegant river front.

Thus, Bordeaux can be said to be an open air XVIIIth century museum. However, it has kept a few older monuments: the basilica of Saint-Michel, with its XVth century tower — a superb belvedere over the city —; the cathedral of Saint-André, the front of which used to be contiguous with the ramparts (the finest doors, dating from the XIIIth and XIVth centuries, are to be found on the flanks); the church of Saint-Seurin, with its XIth century porch and crypt; the medieval door of Grosse-Cloche; Sainte-Croix, a beautiful Romanesque church which was disfigured in the XIXth century. The latin poet Ausone left des-

criptions of the fine squares and luxurious houses of his native town, but Bordeaux does not have many vestiges from the Antiquity: only the ruins of a large third-century amphitheatre called "palais Gallien" are still to be seen, although they were partially destroyed by the Barbarians, and again during the first Empire.

However, Bordeaux is not only a museum city; it is also an active city doubled with an important harbour. The wine trade is still the big business in the vicinity of Médoc, Saint-Émilion, Graves and Sauternes. The Quai des Chartrons (named after an old monastery) is now practically abandoned with its high houses topped with little observatories from which one would watch the sailing and landing of wine-laden ships; the wine-traders, however, are still bound to the city whose name has become an "appellation d'origine contrôlée".

**Médoc and its "châteaux".** A long peninsula stretching between the Gironde and the Atlantic with beaches and pine forests, Médoc is the country of the "châteaux". The word "château", essentially synonymous with a wine-growing farm (like "clos" or "domaine" elsewhere), does not necessarily fit the dictionary definition: it may well have been the dwelling-place of a XVIIIth century nobleman, or an elegant "folly", or a XIXth century rococo manor-house, or even any kind of overwrought architecture without any particular style; yet it may also be a simple house surrounded with vineyards and wine-stores (the *chais*). Everybody in Médoc feel they are lords.

The wine region is entirely different from the coast, with its huge pine forest dotted with lakes and hemmed in by an endless beach. Blurred under a soft light, the rolling hills of the wine-growing part of Médoc are strewn with big villages wearing the names of world-famous wines like Margaux, Saint-Julien and Saint-Estèphe, as well as dozens of solitary châteaux nestling in a clump of trees or watching over their vineyards from the top of a hill. The road numbered D2, truly the wine highway, is the way of access to the estates whose names are on the big-shouldered bottles called "bordelaises". Here is Château Giscours, a splendid Second Empire country-house set in gardens surrounded by impeccably kept vineyards; Château Palmer, a lovely fancy manor-house; Château Margaux, with its ironical peristyle; elegant Château Lanessan with its interesting museum of horse-drawn vehicles; noble Château de Beychevelle, a Louis XV house behind which is hidden a typical — though tiny — fishing harbour; in fact, a simple wharf at the mouth of one of the narrow, reed-lined canals locally called *jalles*.

On the bank of the melancholy estuary Pauillac, a sleepy little town with a big church, boasts of having counted on its territory the largest number of vineyards selected in 1855 — a glorious prize-list which is constantly being referred to. Among the top ones, of world-wide reputation, are château-latour, the boundaries of which have not changed since 1860, mouton-rothschild and lafitte-rothschild. After being owned by the upper class of Bordeaux as well as by a few Englishmen who were traditionally fond of this former possession of the crown (London is the place for the very best bordeaux wines!), Médoc drew the attention of millionaires, and now of the chairmen of the boards of the new multinational firms. Whereas most châteaux have their vineyards and wine-stores close by, one,

*Here is an odd landmark set in the middle of the vineyards: a Roman vestige in the area which produces saint-émilion wine.*

called Grand-Puy-Ducasse, set in the very town of Pauillac, is separated from its estate. The XVIIIth century manor-house harbours a little wine museum; it is also the place of the meetings of the Commanderie du Bontemps de Médoc, a society of wine-growers, traders and local V.I.P.'s.

By Saint-Estèphe, the northernmost wine-growing village, the astonishing manor-house of Cos d'Estournel is a perfect illustration of the mania of the Médocains of yore, for whom the production of a great wine implied an architectural tour de force. Neither château nor folly, nor chartreuse, the strange building looks vaguely like a pagoda, with preposterous pinnacles raised toward the pale grey sky. A copy of the residence of the Sultan of Zanzibar, Cos d'Estournel was built in the XIXth century by an owner who swapped his precious bottles against semi-wild horses. (They still raise horses on the Médoc peninsula, as well as first-rate lamb.) Neither was the man of Cos the first great wine grower from Médoc who personally sought to promote the sale of his own wines abroad. There was a whimsical Chevalier de Rauzan, who personally went to London, where the market prices turned out to be too low for a *grand cru;* so each day he poured a cask of his own wine into the Thames until his panicked customers were prepared to pay a better price for it.

Fort-Médoc has lent its name to a vineyard in Cussac; in this case, however, it is not a château, but a fortress built by Vauban in a superb, isolated location overlooking the Gironde together with Fort Paté, which was built on an island. On the other bank is the formidable citadel of Blaye, which is the other part of the defence system of Bordeaux. Set on a rocky plateau ablaze at sunset, it holds a little town together within its circle of walls, moats, and bastions. From Blaye to the panoramic terrace of Bourg, the Gironde coast road is one of the finest in Bordelais, whether it runs at the level of the water or climbs up the hillsides. One is still in a wine-growing country, not far from Fronsac, Pomerol, and Saint-Émilion.

## The depths of Saint-Émilion.
Set back from the Dordogne (a river flowing from the Massif Central into the Pyrenean Garonne, and on into the Gironde estuary), Saint-Émilion is the strangest of wine-growing capitals. It is partly troglodytic, and the ashlar used to build its strong houses can be confused with the freestone of its hillsides tapped with galleries and hollowed out by large underground halls. In places, the roots of vines can be seen hanging from the vaults. At the edge of the cliff, not far

from an interesting collegiate church of composite style, a high steeple seems to have lost its church. In fact, the spire stands on top of a vast, rustic monolithic sanctuary consisting in three naves carved out of the rock between the IXth and XIIth centuries. The ruins of a chapel nearby is the surviving sign of the homely hermitage where Saint Émilion lived and where he died in 767.

Overlooked by the bulky Château du Roi, which is still surrounded by walls, Saint-Émilion is literally besieged by vineyards. The Romans were fond of the local wine; it is reported that Ausone, the poet and wine-grower, had a house on the estate of what is now Château-Ausone, which is one of the local lordships along with Châteaux Figeac, Cheval-blanc, la Gaffelière, Canon, Pavie, and other top vineyards. At the edge of the Saint-Émilion region, the Pomerol vineyard also produces great wines, aristocratic château-pétrus in particular.

### Between two rivers as between two seas.
The course of both the Dordogne and the Garonne is reversed over several miles by the flowing tide: no more was needed for the triangle of hillsides between the two rivers to be called Entre-deux-Mers (Between-two-Seas). In the space between the two large valleys lies a hilly country crossed by gently murmuring brooks and rivers lined with mills, and covered with meadows, orchards, and tobacco-plantations but also vineyards. The winding roads wander about the lovely countryside or lead to the extraordinary ruins of the former abbey of La Sauve, or yet they take one back to the Garonne which is watched over by Cadillac, Saint-Macaire, La Réole, and Marmande (in Agenais).

On the right bank both Cadillac, with its old *bastide* and its castle of the Dukes of Épernon, and Saint-Macaire look across to the famous vineyards of the left bank, Barsac and Sauternes, which produce incomparable sweet white wines. In the country of golden wines, one never sees parties of wine-harvesters bustling about for a few days, and then breaking up after a cheerful meal. Harvesting drags on for nearly two months because the grapes are gathered, often one by one, only after a tiny mushroom has grown on them. This beneficial parasite has the effect of enhancing the degree of sugar in the grapes as it shrivels them up and starts a mysterious chemical process. With its escort of such excellent sauternes and barsacs as châteaux sigalas-rabaud, climens, coutet, and rayne-vigneau, wealthy (both in taste and in cost!) château-d'yquem looks like a king. The estate

is tended as meticulously as if it were an experimental garden, and you will never see the prestigious name on bottles dating from a mediocre year. In the fine manor-house of Yquem, originally built in the Middle Ages but remodelled under the Renaissance and the XVIIth century, is a court where classical music concerts are held from time to time.

**Where vineyards vie with pines.** The Sauternais is an enclave in the vast wine-growing region of Graves, where both reds and whites are produced at the very edge of the Landes forest. The vine-stocks seem to wage war against the pines, and a vineyard like that of Domaine de Chevalier is beset by woods. The Graves, where people boast of the oldest vineyards in Bordelais, take their name from the siliceous gravel of the soil which is favourable to the wine-plants. The long wine-growing section stretches all the way from the outskirts of Bordeaux to the country of Langon, a little town where many wine-traders live. Some vineyards such as those of Haut-Brion, Pape Clément, and La Mission are now closed in by the tentacular suburbs of Bordeaux. The Graves region harbours historical places like Olivier, Malle, medieval Roquetaillade and above all Labrède. The latter, surrounded by meadows, woods, and vineyards, and set in a pond, was built in the Middle Ages and remodelled between the XVth and XVIIth centuries; it was owned by Montesquieu, a judge and wine-grower who was also the author of *L'Esprit des lois.*

*The Jurade of Saint-Émilion is a seven-century old Wine Brotherhood, whose mission is to carefully control the quality of their* vin fin.

At Château Carbonnieux, the fine manorhouse has retained older parts, and wines are produced on the estate. It has become legendary thanks to the monks who used to tend its vineyards. In spite of the islamic laws prohibiting the use of alcohol, they managed to export their white wine to Turkey by labeling it "mineral water from Carbonnieux". A sultan, probably more in jest than in earnest, is reported to have wondered why people bothered to make wine in a country where water was so good!

**The ocean-like "pignada".** The immense Landes forest, the monotony of which is broken by the undergrowth and by hidden streams, surrounds the Arcachon basin, encroaches upon Médoc, and reaches near Bazas, an old city whose Gothic cathedral, with its highly elaborate front, closes an arcaded square. The "pignada", an artificial forest designed for exploitation, was created during the XIXth century. It has completely changed the sandy moors which used to be marshy and unhealthy, by raising a rampart of slender tree-trunks in front of the shifting sand-hills to which the ocean keeps bringing sand, and which even the plantation of clinging weeds cannot hold. There is still one crumbling mountain, a white hill of sand which keeps moving: called the Dune du Pilat, it is over three hundred feet high, spreads over two miles, and has never stopped progressing towards the interior. It is the sight to be seen in the vicinity of Arcachon, an important seaside resort at the entrance of a large, tide-flooded basin — an interior sea with innumerable channels edged with oyster-beds.

In line with the shore of Médoc as one goes south of Arcachon to the river Adour and to the Basque country, the straight Landes coastline stretches its sand-hills at the edge of the forest, behind the screen of which are hidden the *airials* or clearings

harbouring hamlets. (In the heart of the regional park, a funny little train can take the visitor from Sabres to the model *airial* of Marquèze, which has become an open-air museum.) Several seaside resorts are currently growing under the watchful eye of the "Mission Aquitaine", an official organism which is responsible for the basic facilities and keeps town-planning under control. Soulac-sur-Mer, Montalivet-les-Bains (the Mecca of naturists) and Lacanau-Océan are in Médoc, whereas the southern resorts are Biscarosse-Plage, Mimizan-Plage, Vieux-Boucau and the twin resorts of Hossegor and Capbreton.

The beaches are hollowed out into pools called *baïnes* and beaten by the ocean, the waves of which are favourable to surfers. There are miles and miles of beaches so empty in many places as to be paradise on earth for those keen on allover suntans; swimming, however, is carefully watched over wherever it is permitted. The lovers of the peaceful breast-stroke and of safe boat-racing prefer the large, pine-circled, almost windless lakes which are connected together through little canals or which overflow into the ocean through channels hidden under lovely undergrowth. At Hossegor, a large resort scattered over a large pine plantation, the lake has been tide-flooded ever since a channel was dug out in the former bed of wayward Adour. In the same way was an artificial lake recently created at Vieux-Boucau under the aegis of the Mission.

Next to the Landes of the forest, or *airials,* and of *gemmage* (the tapping of trees for resin) are other Landes, rustic, hospitable, where Indian corn is grown and poultry bred: yellow chickens, ducks and geese fattened for their livers. These places are called Orthe, Peyrehorade, Sorde-l'Abbaye, Arthous and Hastingue, and there are the gentle hills of the Chalosse, and tiny Tursan where vines are still clinging.

*An endless forest of maritime pines (opposite); the mountain-high sand-* *dune of Le Pilat, and the soft outlines of the Arcachon basin (above): the Landes stretch along the Ocean.*

# the Pays basque

WHEREAS THE LANDES are Gascon, the Pays basque is... Basque, and will not be deterred from it. It is a little nation, sharing the *département* of Pyrénées-Atlantiques with Béarn, and faithful to its mysterious language, *eskuara,* which has nothing in common with any of the other European idioms. South of the Adour the people are *Eskualdunak* (or *Euskaldunak*), which means "those who can speak Basque", and who understand their brothers from beyond the Spanish frontier, as Eskual-Herria extends to both France and Spain. The irony of history is that the very name of the Basques is not Basque: like "Gascon", it recalls the Vascon invaders who settled in the Southwest in the VIIth century.

A highly individualized land, the Pays basque has been somewhat corrupted by tourism, especially along its rocky coast-line. With its colourful harbour, its old streets, and the church where Louis XIV was married, Saint-Jean-de-Luz has retained its quaint character, whereas Biarritz is an international resort, with new buildings soaring in disorder from among startling monuments dating back to the Second Empire and the *Belle Époque.* As a holiday resort, it confronts the ocean with a curved beach made even wider by the low tide, with a beautiful, steep promontory called L'Atalaye, which is carved with winding walks and flights of steps, and with the grey, crumbling cliffs of the Côte des Basques. As opposed to international Biarritz, Bayonne is half-Basque, half-Gascon; with star-shaped fortifications by Vauban, it stretches its embankments along the river Adour and is cut through by the smaller Nive.

The French Pays basque, which is made quite green by its warm, rather rainy climate, is traditionally divided into three equally charming parts: the coastal Labourd, where the white, half-timbered houses with their dissymetrical roofs fit the uneven setting admirably, the Basse-Navarre, with its rugged surface and its varied landscapes; and, wedged between the two, the Soule, consisting in the valley of one little river, the Saison. Aïnhoa, Espelette, Itxassou, Bidarray and many other villages with strange names are all extremely enticing, but the sight to be seen in the inte-

rior is definitely Saint-Jean-Pied-de-Port, an historical city where the pilgrims would stop on their way to Compostelle before walking up to the passe (« port ») of Ibaneta and down to Roncevaux.

The Soule, which is the easternmost part of the Basque provinces, is perhaps the most unfamiliar too, with its curious "trinitarian" bell-towers (with three bell-turrets). The forest of Iraty is a vast, cool expanse of trees and fresh water. Nearby is the spectacular canyon of Kakouéta, the "Pyrenean Verdon", and the Romanesque church of

*At the mouth of the Nivelle on the bay of Biscaye, Saint-Jean-de-Luz is made lively by the tunny boats sailing in and out of the harbour (opposite, left).*

Saint-Engrâce. The Soule is contiguous to Béarn, at the edge of which stands the unusual church of L'Hôpital-Saint-Blaise, a stern XIIth century monument with an octogonal steeple and a mixture of Romanesque and Moorish styles.

# Béarn

BÉARN, WHICH WAS HENRY IV's home-land — or rather kingdom — is a combination of clear water mount-ain-torrents called *gaves,* of mountains peopled with *izards* (wild goats), of closed valleys, rounded hills and small plains, and vineyards, grass-land and forests. This mosaic of agricultural and pastoral lands

*Over the centuries, the Basque country has retained its traditions and its festivals, such as their graceful "apple dance" (above) or the playing of txis-tulari (opposite).*

was an industrial desert until the Lacq gas-fields (now almost exhausted) were discovered. It spreads over approximately two thirds of the Pyrénées-Atlantiques. Between Bigorre, which is highlighted by the pilgrimages to Lourdes, the city of the Virgin; Armagnac with its world-famous spirit; Tursan; Chalosse, and the high Pyrenean peaks, Béarn has preserved an identity forged over centuries of independence: it became part of the crown of France only under Louis XIII, the son of Henry IV who himself was a son of Béarn and became the king of France after the bloody Wars of Religion.

An entity in itself within *Occitan* France, clearly set apart from Pays basque and endeavouring to keep its own dialect (a form of *Gascon*), Béarn is made up of a variety of sub-regions; it is nonetheless characterized by its habitat — strong houses topped with huge, steep roofs. After Orthez, an old city with a bridge over the dark brown *gave*, Pau became its capital. A beautiful city facing the endless mountain panorama, Pau consists in old houses somewhat marred by the excessive

restorations of the XIXth century. In it are to be seen the turtleshell which was used as a cradle for Henry IV, tapestries, and very fine furniture; and one may conjure up characters like Gaston de Foix, called Phébus or "the Brilliant", Marguerite d'Angoulême, a poetess and the friend of free spirits, and Jeanne d'Albret, an opinionated Calvinist who became the mother of Henry IV.

In Oloron-Sainte-Marie, the church of Sainte-Croix, the oldest Romanesque sanctuary in Béarn, stands higher than Sainte-Marie, the former cathedral with a renowned portal. The town, a combination of two cities which used to be extremely jealous of their own autonomy, controls access to the deep valley of Aspe and to the road of the Somport. Running almost parallel to it is the valley of Ossan, leading up to the border-pass of Le Pourtalet. This valley, once a tiny autonomous republic celebrated by the Romantics, is the way of access to the ice-cold lake of Artouste which is at an altitude of over 6,000 feet. A cable-car takes visitors over from an extraordinary little mountain train running on a narrow-gauge line overlooking dizzy steeps.

# *Bigorre*

O**N THE SLOPES OF THE PYRÉNÉES**, the mountain-range of Bigorre, whose high, enclaved valleys are still the scene of the age-old custom of moving flocks called *transhumance*, constitutes, together with Béarn and Pays basque, a

rather heterogeneous region wich local people call the "Three B's". It is mostly pastoral, with many sheep pens; high above Bagnères towers the Pic du Midi de Bigorre which is nearly 9,000 feet high, while at the foot of the mountain Lourdes, the marian city known the world over, attracts thousands of pilgrims and millions of visitors: the modern underground basilica can hold 20,000 of them. The history of Lourdes began in 1858, when Bernadette Soubirous, a miller's daughter, saw the Virgin as the Immaculate Conception. It is a strange, impressive, and sometimes painful sight to see the innumerable tourists lingering among the souvenir shops while the sick hoping for recovery pray in front of the Grotto of the Miracle, in the church of the Rosary or in the upper part of the basilica with its countless ex-votos...

Being at a crossroads, Lourdes is a permanent invitation to many excursions to Tarbes and the Lannemezan plateau, to the pass of Aubisque (the panoramic road is beautiful), and to the grand « cirque de Gavarnie » with its huge tiers and immense walls.

## Historical landmarks

*The Basque country, Béarn and the county of Toulouse had a separate history. The Basque country, which was occupied only briefly by the Romans, remained autonomous under a partial English administration and then under the Ancien Régime (the French government until the Revolution). Basse-Navarre, one of the three provinces included in the Basque country, was part of Navarre, an independent kingdom. The Basque country pushed aside the nobility and administered itself in a rather democratic manner. Béarn was a free nation in spite of its princes' ties of vassalage. It remained neutral during the Hundred Years' War and had its Golden Age in the XIVth century. The Béarnais viscounts, who became kings of Navarre through a marriage, lost the part of Navarre situated on the other side of the Pyrenees to Ferdinand the Catholic, who annexed it. However, they retained their title. One of them, Henri d'Albret, became Henri IV at the end of the Wars of Religion: therefore, the kings of France were also those of Navarre. Joined to the crown by the Vert Galant (Henry IV), Béarn was permanently incorporated into France by his son Louis XIII.*

*As for the powerful county of Toulouse, battered by the cruisade against the Albigenses in the beginning of the XIIIth century, it did not follow in the footsteps of Aquitaine, of which it was the capital during the Carolingian period. In 1271 it became part of the kingdom.*

*"The most mysterious achievement by the most mysterious architect", as Victor Hugo called it, the Cirque de Gavarnie is shown here with its snow-capped tiers rising up to 4,500 feet.*

# *Armagnac*

To THE NORTH OF BIGORRE can be found the green hills of Armagnac: a mosaic of meadows, vineyards and groves strewn with big, low farmhouses. At Auch, the old city and the cathedral watch over the Gers, whose floods are formidable. This region has many hot springs, some of which are not even exploited; and it has a prestigious roving ambassador: the alcoholic drink bearing its name. Also produced in the eastern Landes, in the vicinity of Villeneuve-de-Marsan and Labastide, armagnac is a delectable brandy necessitating a long ageing in barrels of white oak. Whereas it is so rough as to be almost undrinkable when straight out of the still, it mellows in the barrels so as to acquire an unmatched bouquet.

Like other parts of the Southwest, Armagnac is covered with *bastides,* or villages built geometrically around a square with arcades by the kings of France and England when they fought over Aquitaine. These were centres of settlement in underpeopled areas, and they served as strongholds as well, so that from them one may still infer the location of the moving frontiers of the time: most of the French bastides are north of the Dordogne river.

On the border between Armagnac and Quercy, apart from Aquitaine, the Toulouse region is linked with Bordelais by a water thoroughfare, the Garonne; yet it is even more turned towards the Mediterranean. A fine and lively brick city, Toulouse retains a great deal of charm in spite of its being clogged with traffic. The Saint-Sernin basilica — the finest Romanesque church in the south of France —, the impressive Gothic

*The memory of the historic turmoil in the duchy of Aquitaine still lingers over the bastides of Gascogne. Nowadays, only covered markets such as the one shown above, in Auvillar, are busy. Also eventful was the destiny of Toulouse, the capital of Haut-Languedoc, whose Saint-Sernin basilica (opposite) reveals the mystical spirit of the romanesque period.*

church of the Jacobins, and the very rich museum of the Augustins are musts, but nobody can be familiar with Toulouse without lingering on Place Esquérol and in the little streets lined with medieval or Renaissance houses.

*During the Middle Ages, Saint-Bertrand-de-Comminges, a stop on the way to Saint-Jacques-de-Compostelle at the foot of the Pyrenees, was an important Christian sanctuary. Although partially rebuilt in the XIVth century, the cathedral of Notre-Dame has kept fine romanesque vestiges, among which is a donjon with a wooden gallery and a cloister opening on the outside (opposite).*

# Quercy

NORTH OF CORDES, a unique medieval city enclosed within four walls, and of Montauban, an old town built on a terrace overlooking the Tarn river, stretches Quercy, an historical region now practically associated with the Lot *département*, on the border of Périgord. The river winds its way between upper and lower Quercy, beneath cliffs topped with villages of another time like Saint-Cirq-Lapopie, or proud castles like Mercuès. Its swift stream with many ephemeral whirlpools flows around the age-old cathedral and city of Cahors, and glides under the Valentré bridge, a medieval military construction with a unique shape: tradition has it that Satan helped the architect bristle it up with towers and battlements.

In Quercy are to be seen many *causses,* which are uneven and barren plateaux interspersed with green valleys often fragrant with lavender; the *causses* are hollowed by pits, one of which, named Padirac,

*In the heart of France barren cliffs called* causses, *deep gorges and winding valleys make up dramatic landscapes* (top of page, right: *the Détroits in the gorges of the Tarn*). *Men settled in sites where they could be* safe from attack, whether on top of rocky spurs, as in Saint-Cirq-Lapopie (opposite), *or at the foot of steep hills, as in La Roque-Gageac, on the banks of the Dordogne* (above).

can be said to be as famous as Chambord, Mont-Saint-Michel, or Chartres. Four lifts take one down the dizzy chasm to a weird landscape in which, from flat metallic boats, one can see the underground river and harbour, waterfalls, lakes, and a forest of chalk-stones with opal colours. Quite different although no less striking is Rocamadour, a holy city clinging to a high cliff in which are inlaid many sanctuaries where pilgrims would flock during the Middle Ages. Beneath an eagle's nest with a heavily restored castle, medieval Rocamadour is a challenge to the laws of gravitation, as it always seems to be on the verge of crumbling down into the Alzou, a rivulet reflecting a site which is all the finer for being seen in the morning sun.

*On the way to Saint-Jacques-de-Compostelle, the Romanesque abbey-church of Conques stands overlooking one of the most picturesque sites in Rouergue (left page). The storiated capitals of the cloister at Moissac (above) tell us about the time when the pilgrims stopped in the monastery. The chapel of Saint-Michel in Rocamadour (opposite is shown a detail of one of the outside frescoes) stands in one of the most popular places of pilgrimage.*

# Périgord

THE COURSE OF THE WINDING DOR-
DOGNE, sometimes swift and sometimes lazy, begins in the higher
parts of Quercy; then the superb valley
delineates one of the most beautiful itineraries in Périgord, whose limits are approximately those of the Dordogne *département.* This is a many-faceted region, with
a thousand manor-houses and castles, pre-
historic caves, fatted geese and truffles; the
colour of the vegetation, however, explains
why it is divided — somewhat arbitrarily —
between black Périgord (centre and east)
and green Périgord (north), to which should
be added the district around Bergerac as
well as smaller, local areas.

Haughty fortresses, proud castles, country seats, citadels and bastides are to be
found all over Périgord, just as churches
and abbeys. To these impressive tokens of
pre-revolutionary France, all of them admirably integrated, must be added many pre-
historic landmarks, the shelters and caves
of the Dordogne and especially of the Vézère
(a river nicknamed «the axis of prehistory»), which tell the tale of *Homo Sapiens*
— the way he improved on his own tools,
perfecting his hunting methods, discover-
ing art as he cut into soft chalk and painted
the walls of his caves. The history of
Périgord began some forty thousand years
before Christ!

The statue of a primitive man watches
over Les Eyzies, the capital of prehistory in
the vicinity of which are many fields, shelters under overhanging rocks, and decorated caves. The cave of Lascaux, a fabulous museum of mural art, which was
accidentally discovered in 1940 in Monti-
gnac, has now been closed to the public
because of the "green germ" caused by the
crowds of visitors, which damaged the sty-
lised compositions, the colours of which
had kept their brightness until then.

In Sarlat, the Middle Ages, the Renaissance, and the classical period are still to
be seen in the high-gabled houses, the
medieval fronts, the arcades and archways,
and in a rather heterogeneous church. The
white city is a charming sight, especially
on a market day (Saturday). In the vicinity, dozens of manor-houses and country

*The castle of Bonaguil, with its stem-shaped keep and its honey-hued walls, was a fortress built in the XIIIth century on the border of Quercy and improved upon in the Renais-sance by a belated feudal squire, Bérenger de Roquefeuil. It repel-led all attacks, but was demolished during the Revolution.*

seats are to be seen either withdrawn from or overlooking the river, whose ample bends under overhanging rocks are locally called *cingles.* It is a must to cross over it near the Romanesque church of Cénac so as to discover Domme, a high-perched, fortified bastide the esplanade of which offers an overlook on the valley and a panorama of « black » Périgord.

Périgueux, the capital of Périgord and the *préfecture* of Dordogne, nestles in a bend of the Isle, in the water of which are to be seen reflections of the old house fronts and of the striking cupolas of the large cathedral of Saint-Font (XIIth century, heavily restored); this huge and cold Byzantine-looking church stands on the edge of an old area with paved alleys and picturesque houses. Under the name of Vésone, Périgueux was once an important Gallo-Roman city, and it has kept a few vestiges dating from the beginnings of our era in the vicinity of the former cathedral of Saint-Étienne-de-la-Cité, particularly the strange and stately tower of Vésone.

Going up the Dronne, a little river whose swift waters lap at mills and green valleys, one catches sight of the massive ramparts of the castle of Bourdeilles clinging to the edge of the cliff, and then of Brantôme, with its willows weeping over the reflection of a long, XVIIIth century abbey and of its original Romanesque steeple.

*Périgord, a prehistoric shrine, conceals many vestiges, particularly in the vicinity of Eyzies-de-Tayac, where is to be seen the cave of Font-de-Gaume, hollowed out by deep galleries painted with frescoes (above).*

# *Limousin*

U NDER AN OFTEN CLOUDY SKY, Limousin is contiguous to Périgord. Apparently originating in Massif central with its quick rivers, it stretches its woods and meadows in a series of rolling plateaux where cattle, sheep, and horses are raised. In higher Limousin, the severest and most inhospitable landscapes are gradually changing with the planting of resinous trees in land formerly used for grazing sheep. Thus does the well watered Millevaches plateau owe to foresters its surprising metamorphosis.

Limoges, the capital of Limousin, has developed on the right bank of the steep-banked Vienne, spanned by two old bridges. Like Périgueux, Limoges owes its existence to the union of two formerly independent cities, the limits of which can still be perceived. The cathedral has a wonderful flamboyant portal, but Limoges is above all the "city of chinaware", with dinner sets exported all over the world. (In fact, it all began with enamel, both *cloisonné* and *champlevé.*) The best way to get acquainted with both enamel and chinaware is to visit the town museum and the Adrien-Dubouché national museum, which is devoted to china from all over the world.

*The little medieval city of Collonges in lower Limousin, with its red sandstone, its fortified gates and its old houses among trees, is no less than an open-air museum: shown here is the former Hotel de la Ramade de Friac.*

# *Languedoc*

**W**ITHOUT A CAPITAL LETTER, "le midi" is only a cardinal point. With a capital M as in Méditerranée, however, "le Midi" is the south-eastern part of France: Languedoc and Provence lumped together — a vast sunny region with a long seashore stretching from Spain to Italy, on both sides of the delta of the Rhône. The lack of unity in the southern regions, the sharp contrasts in the landscapes, an excessive or insufficient degree of industrialization, the endless problems raised by viticulture, the realities of everyday life, the fears of ecologists — all these melt away when you hear the magic word, the two brief syllables which conjure up mirages such as ruffled-up palm-trees signalling deep bays; golden splashes of mimosas in the midst of February; silvery olive-groves and fields

covered with lavender; *garrigues* (moors) full of chirring cicadas; warm-water gulfs and secret *calanques* (coves) — and travel-agency holidays. Even if it fails to satisfy either geographers or historians, the very word "Midi" enhances the Northerners' dreams whenever they feel oppressed by their low, grey skies.

You go "down" to the Midi, and yet nobody knows where it begins. Some spot it wherever the first pink-red roofs replace slates and *lauzes* (a regional name for slabs of mica schist). This is going too fast, since Mâconnais and Beaujolais are southern only to people from northern Bourgogne. Others see a change in Vienne. Others again find the door to the South in Valence, with the first lines of upright cypresses. One can also wait until

one sees the first olive-trees, or else consider that the Midi begins in the vicinity of Montélimar, where the nameless northern wind becomes the mistral, the better to hustle whatever clouds cling to the blue sky.

From the easternmost jagged tops of the Pyrénées to Mercantour, a high scraggy mountain mass in the Franco-Italian Alps, the Midi is characterized by the Mediterranean climate: dry, hot summers, quite warm winters, precocious and fragrant springs, and few — though sometimes violent — rains. Such a climate may explain why so many tourists are drawn to the region and to its warm sea, rather than to its thousand beautiful sights and cities. It used to be fashionable to spend the winter there; nowadays, the Midi is crowded in summer-

*Red Albi, built in brick from Langue-doc (preceding pages), has kept a masterpiece of Southern Gothic architecture, the stately fortress-cathedral*

*of Sainte-Cécile, whose beauty is enhanced by the presence of the Palais de la Berbie opposite the uneven arches of the Pont-Vieux over the Tarn.*

*Carcassonne, which was nicknamed "the virgin of Languedoc" because it was supposed to be impregnable, is the largest single fortress in Europe. Rising out of vineyards and*

*surrounded by double walls, it used to be the siege of religious, civilian, and military authorities. Today, travellers can loiter along the covered, battlemented rounds way.*

time, as if people wanted to be sure to get a maximum of sunshine in one of the most famous sun-tanning places in Europe. Indeed, the rate of sunshine is 90 % (although there are accidents!), including autumn.

**The fragrant garrigues.** The main effect of such a climate is a typically Mediterranean vegetation, with green oaks, cork-oaks and pine-trees, fragrant bushes full of drunken bees, vineyards and orchards.

Barren mountains shut the horizon with wild, chaotic slopes of a stern beauty; cypress-trees grown as protection against the wind as well as screens of *canisses* (reed-mats) shade and shelter the market-gardens. In spots, the bright rocks are interspersed with tufts of fragrant herbs where sheep and goats graze. In other places, they give way to the moors or *garrigues* covered with rosemary, thyme (locally called *farigoule*), sage and many other aromatic plants which are used to flavour dishes already pungent with fruity olive-oil and strong garlic. The Midi, however, is more varied than Northerners usually think. Heaths covered with brush-wood and resonant with the chirping of insects alternate with vineyards, the fertile fields of Comtat Venaissin (the best land in Vaucluse) with the rice-swamps of Camargue and the rocky desert of La Crau... Even the coast is far from uniform as it offers long beaches, marshes, a thousand coves and large bays.

The language spoken in the Midi is the "langue d'oc" which was used by the troubadors of yore and by the heroes of Frédéric Mistral, who originated a widespread regional literary movement called the *Félibrige*. In Languedoc as well as in Provence, people have a way of making the French language sing, and they show a great deal of faithfulness to their own, rich dialects — or they learn them. There is undoubtedly an Occitan language as well as an Occitan culture, which are resistant, even occasionally flourishing anew. Not all children can speak it, but many keep the hearty accent and the verbal nimbleness which are always a surprise to people speaking the "langue d'oïl". There is even a touch of commiseration in the latter being described here as speaking « pointu » — or with a northern accent.

### Historical landmarks

*Languedoc, formerly the property of the counts of Toulouse, was made part of France in the XIIIth century after the bloody crusade against the Albigenses. During the Hundred Years' War, it proved its loyalty to the crown by being the first to support Charles VII. Heavily infiltrated by Protestantism, it suffered greatly during the Religious Wars, which deeply divided its people.*

**Old towns versus new resorts.** Languedoc is an old region where memories of the *Albigeois* (or *Cathares*), those heretics who were exterminated by the end of a ruthless crusade in the XIIIth century, still linger. It varies considerably in scope accord-

*Languedoc has the best-kept vestiges of all Roman Gaul, among which are the Pont du Gard, an harmoniously shaped, almost intact aqueduct, and the famous Maison carrée in Nîmes,* *whose charming fragility is only apparent since it is belied by its endurance. Its thirty corinthian columns are a token of the hellenistic influence.*

92

ing to whether it is considered historically or geographically. Toulouse was the capital of Languedoc before the Revolution, but the region is now limited to its Mediterranean section, between the Corbières mounts and Camargue, the wild, beautiful Cévennes and the sea. Landscapes are varied, from *garrigues* and vineyards to barren mountains or to fertile basins, all strewn with golden cities and feudal ruins. The features of the coast have recently been chan-

ged under the aegis of the agency for regional development: whereas mile after mile of it used to be deserted except by mosquitoes, it was drained, bulldozed, remodeled and covered with concrete, thus becoming an important centre of attraction for tourists in the span of ten years. However, this metamorphosis (which has left many places untouched) has had little effect on the highly individual character of the people, who are *Occitan* both in their hearts

and in their language. Languedocians are independent and proud, occasionally quick-tempered; they will fight bitterly over their rights as well as over their individuality and their vineyards; they feel a natural sympathy for their neighbours, the people of the wild Grands Causses, who are opposed to the spreading of a military base over the barren lands of Larzac, where only sheep can graze.

Nîmes is the door to Languedoc and the *préfecture* of Gard. Its amphitheatre, which dates back to the first century B.C., its famous Maison Carrée and its Roman ruins are surrounded by garrigues. Two trips ought to be taken from Nîmes: one to the Pont du Gard, a stunning Roman aqueduct, and one to Aigues-Mortes, a melancholy city enclosed in perfectly kept walls.

Montpellier, the *préfecture* of Hérault, is a city which is enlivened by its student population and enlightened by gardens and by the harmonious Promenade du Peyrou. It has an incomparable group of XVIIth and XVIIIth century buildings, and it can boast of one of the richest art galleries in France (the Fabre Museum), and of a medical school founded in 1221. Pézenas although much smaller, is highly picturesque, and owns an extraordinary combination of old houses. A motorway now runs between Béziers, one of the meccas of rugby, Narbonne, a closed labyrinth of winding streets, and Carcassonne, the formidable fortified wall of which was begun in the Vth century by the Visigoths. Behind the circle of walls is a city from another time, a castle and the church of Saint-Nazaire; quite distinct is the lower town, which was planned as early as the XIIIth century.

*Catalonia was deeply influenced by the spirit of mysticism which impelled southern Romanesque art in the Middle Ages. Overlooking a valley of the Conflent river stands the elegant, crenellated bell-tower of the abbey of Saint-Michel (above), built over a cloister which was reconstructed in part, with its capitals depicting picturesque figures. The abbey of Saint-Martin-du-Canigou, which was recently restored, is representative of the Roussillon romanesque architecture which was influenced by the Saracens; the result was odd and mystical, with a touch of naïvety here and there — as shown in this detail of a capital symbolizing sin (right).*

Before it reaches Spain, the motorway, which is overloaded with traffic during the summer holidays, runs along the vine-growing region of Corbières, a chalk bastion standing against the Pyrénées. This is a country with many Romanesque churches, and it is covered with *cistes* (rock-roses), lavender and broom wherever vineyards have not taken over. Perpignan, the capital of Roussillon (a province which, after belonging to Spain, joined France in the XVIIth century), is a former stronghold watched over by an enormous citadel which encloses the medieval castle of the Kings of Majorca. It is a lively, pleasant city the aspect of which, in its most historical parts, recalls the XVIIIth century. It controls the end of the Têt valley, which one must use in order to reach the sunny skiing centre of Font-Romeu, where the amount of sunshine is so remarkable as to have justified the building of a solar furnace long before the energy crisis.

**Planning the coastal area.** The Mediterranean coast between Camargue and Spain has always been deserted and inhospitable, consisting in long, sandy stretches, wind-beaten dunes, ponds and lakes and other "mosquito nests" — with too few natural shelters. Tourists would flock to Sète, a pretty town with canals and a "cimetière marin" made famous by Paul Valéry, or to Narbonne, Canet-Plage, Argelès-sur-Mer, Collioure (of which Matisse and Dufy were so fond) and Banyuls-sur-Mer, a fishing harbour set in vineyards. Everything changed under the impulse of an interdepartmental agency whose mission has consisted in promoting under strict control a new Côte d'Azur. The longest beaches on the coast (100 miles of fine sand) are now settled with new "touristic units" in alternation with older resorts and separated by natural spaces either kept intact or newly forested. Concrete is common to all of these holiday resorts built in the midst of the desert, as well as to the sailing and yachting harbours now offering thousands of moorings — and yet the architecture is far from being uniform: Port-Camargue is characterized by cubistic tangles, La Grande-Motte by strange, futuristic pyramids, Cap d'Agde and Port-Leucate-Port-Barcarès by traditional Mediterranean styles, Guissan by curiously bent roofs not far from a strange huddle of chalets on posts. As the danger was to see the newly developed coastal area cut from its back country, the agency and the local authorities have been trying to establish a symbiosis between holiday-makers and local residents.

*With its battlemented platform and its Lombard arcadings, the bell-tower of Saint-Martin-du-Canigou stands on the rocky side of Mont Canigou, which provided marble for the Romanesque architecture built in the South.*

# Provence

**S**OUTH OF ARLES, the Rhône valley, which is the main way of access to the Midi, spreads out into a vast, marshy delta: called Camargue, it is a separate universe between Languedoc and Provence. Upstream, the river is quieted down by a series of dams, so that it is full of majesty as it reaches the former Orange County, which used to be the possession of the Nassau family who are still on the throne of Holland. A few miles away from the river, Orange is a city with charming little squares overlooked by a formidable Roman amphitheatre where important artistic events still take place. There are Roman vestiges everywhere in this region, particularly in Vaison-la-Romaine, a city stamped with an ancient seal — and a paradise for archaeologists. In it are to be found a theatre dating back to the beginning of our era and considerable excavations keep company with treasures from the Romanesque period, and a picturesque upper town with archi-

tectural legacies from the Renaissance and from the XVIIIth century.

South of Vaison is the "Giant of Provence", the Mont Ventoux, an advanced spur of the Alps, whose slopes are a memorable test for the racing cyclists engaged in the "Tour de France". The 6,273 feet high Ventoux, which was climbed by Petrarch, is one of the finest belvederes in the south of France: it overlooks the Comtat Venaissin, a former possession of the Popes which officially became French under the Revolution. (With the exception of the County of Nice, the annexation of which took place in 1860, the rest of Provence had become French by the end of the XVth century.) Often whipped by the mistral, which hedges of cypress-trees try to fight, the Comtat is a fertile region irrigated by many canals. The sun and the Durance have turned it into the garden of Provence. Carpentras, its former capital, now called the "cité du berlingot" (a boiled sweet), rules over an agricultural and vine-growing count-

*Old villages in which every stone tells a story, steep alleyways lined with colourful housefronts, peaceful squares with murmuring fountains (opposite is shown the village of Flassan, at the foot of Mont Ventoux) — such is contemporary Provence, which remains faithful to its own past and traditions (above, a celebration in Arles).*

ry. South of it, in a section devoted to market gardening, with many hothouses and orchards, Cavaillon has always had a romance with Luberon, the enchanted mountain where one still remembers the Vaudois, heretics who were slaughtered by the order of François I in the XVIth century.

Petrarch, the humanist, a poet and historian from Italy, who was a great figure in Avignon in the XIVth century, was particularly fond of retiring to the green oasis of Fontaine-de-Vaucluse where he could dream about beautiful Laure. Nearby is the mysterious and famous fountain, a spectacular resurgence which was explored in vain by Captain Cousteau and an underwater robot called Télénaute. Gordes, an old village clinging to the edge of the Vaucluse plateau, in the midst of a barren landscape dotted with round huts made of dry stone and called *bories*, was almost in ruins by the end of World War II. Much was done to save it by Victor Vasarely, the painter whose name is also associated with Aix-en-Provence, and who restored the XVIth century castle, a fine Renaissance architectural piece, which he turned into a living museum where his own, varied works are on show. Nearby, in a peaceful valley, the abbey of Sénanque, a masterpiece of unornamented architecture, now harbours an exhibition on the Sahara. It was abandoned by the monks in 1969. Along with Silvacane and Le Thoronet, Sénanque is one of the "three Cistercian sisters » of Provence.

**Deep Provence and the city of the Popes.** Standing apart from the Alps, the Lure

mountain, which is very steep on its north side, slopes gently down southward to the Forcalquier region, where harshness and sweetness, charm and melancholy are blended. This is another Provence, strewn with

*Nestled in the hollow of a solitary little valley fragrant with lavender, the abbey of Sénanque owes its symmetry as well as the perfect stonework of its architecture to the Cistercian Romanesque style. Opposite is shown the dormitory, whose thick walls sheltered the monks from both cold and hot weathers.*

scattered little *mas* painted pink, and still isolated in spite of tourists: the deep Provence of novelist Jean Giono, who was born in Manosque.

The impressively deep and narrow canyon of the river Verdon is one of the finest sights to be seen in Provence, but the river has been quieted down by important dams. It runs into the Durance, a Haute Provence river which has also been dammed before it flows into the Rhône south of Avignon. The city of the Popes, with its network of narrow streets, is sheltered behind an uninterrupted belt of crenellated ramparts. The city, which is the colour of dry leaves, is a must in Provence; it has been the seat of the famous theatre festival created by Jean Vilar ever since 1947.

"He who has not seen Avignon under the Popes has seen nothing", wrote Alphonse Daudet, a native of Nîmes who wrote about Provence with both whimsicality and tenderness. With its old houses huddled within the walls and overlooked by a rocky belvedere, the *préfecture* of Vaucluse is still radiant with an old halo: it was the siege of the Popes for the whole of the XIVth century, and it remained a possession of the Holy See until 1791. The city is dominated by the massive Palais des Papes, an elegant Gothic fortress with high towers where Benoît XII's Palais-Vieux adjoins Clément VI's Palais-Neuf. It is scattered with venerable churches and noble townhouses,

### Historical landmarks

*Provence, formerly populated by Ligurians, became* Provincia romana, *from where it gets its name. During the feudal period, it grew and shrank in size, due to marriages, inheritances and treaties, and its history is particularly complicated. It belonged to the dukes of Anjou (Good King René established his residence there in 1470), then to René's nephew, and soon thereafter to Louis XI. Aside from the Comtat Venaissin (which belonged to the papacy from 1274 to 1791; seven popes and two antipopes lived in Avignon, which was under the legates' rule until the Revolution), the Principality of Monaco and the territories of Savoie remained independent. The county of Nice was joined to France in 1860, when Menton and Roquebrune were broken off from the ministate of Monaco. Tende and La Brigue remained part of Italy until 1947.*

*A dizzy cut in the plateaux of Haute Provence, the grand canyon of Verdon (upper left) thrusts its grey-and-pink cliffs upward to a height of between 900 and 2,100 feet above the green ribbon of the river, which winds its way along 15 miles in this dramatic setting.*

and is proud of the art treasures housed in the Calvet Museum. In the XIXth century, a thoroughfare was built which cuts across the city before reaching the Place de l'Horloge. Always busy, the latter is turned into a *souk* during the Festival (July and the beginning of August). The bridge made famous by the nursery rhyme ("Sur le pont d'Avignon...") and which, in reality, is called Saint-Bénézet, dates from the end of the XIIth century; only four arches of it have survived, but it still bears a chapel.

The Rhône flows between Avignon and Villeneuve-lès-Avignon, an old Languedoc city with a restored charterhouse; then it bends round the thyme-fragrant hills of La Montagnette which, according to Daudet, was the training-ground of his hero Tarta-rin de Tarascon. This pseudo-mountain, where almond, cypress and pine-trees grow, can be considered as the essence of Provence; it seems to be the vanguard of the Alpilles — a little, very low though quite jagged range made of pale chalk hollowed out into narrow gorges and grottoes locally called *baumes*. On the edge of the Alpilles range is the charming, sleepy little town

*Avignon* (above), *an immutable landmark under the soft light of Comtat Venaissin, has retained the untouched symbols of the time when it was the siege of popery.*

*Les Baux-de-Provence* (following pages) : *at the foot of a ruined feudal castle, the dwellings of a modest village mingle with the vestiges of a ruined city.*

of Saint-Rémy-de-Provence. Nearby is an ancient site with a perfectly well-kept mausoleum and a Roman arch. Harsh in places but often fascinating, the landscape can hardly be called tragic except in the tortured paintings of Vincent Van Gogh, who fought against madness and went to a local clinic in 1889-1890.

Between the Durance and the Rhône rivers, not far from Maillane where Frédéric Mistral was born, Saint-Rémy offers a hundred walks in the Provence of *la farigoule* (the local name for thyme), of cicadas and of "le sous-préfet aux champs", a character half civil servant, half poet invented by Daudet. The eagle's nest of Les Baux-de-Provence (from *baou*, a rock) has constructions which can be confused with the white or red (from bauxite) stones of a landscape carved by erosion and hollowed out to quarries as big as cathedrals — a truly cubistic labyrinth in which Jean Cocteau made his film *Orpheus*. Under moonlight, it is a mineral world which brings to mind Dante's poem. The city, with its ruined castle and ramparts, seems to have been carved in the rock. It was entirely preserved thanks to the association for historical monuments, which has taken perfect care of it. It stretches its Renaissance houses and its ruins to the edge of the deserted plateau where the donjon and dovecote of the demolished fortress stand out. The top of the promontory allows a dazzling panorama under a hard blue sky: hill after hill covered with wind-tortured pines, Fontvieille whose windmill inspired Daudet, Montmajour and its massive abbey, the flat rice-growing country, Arles and the steppes of La Crau... This dazzling, monotonous stretch, bumpy with big stones hot with sunshine, incredibly dry wherever there is no irrigation, is a separation between the Alpilles and quite another Provence — that

of Fos-sur-Mer and of the Étang de Berre, where a formidable industrial complex has been built in relation with the "Europort" of Fos-Marseille, in which the biggest oil and ore tankers can dock.

**The flat country of the nomads.** The Rhône bends eastward and flows between the theatrical castle of Tarascon and the ruined fortress of Beaucaire, a sleepy Languedocian town, and then on to Arles, which is at once Roman, medieval, and profoundly Provençal — an open air museum whose stones tell an age-old story. The city whose name is associated with Van Gogh has kept admirable vestiges of its past: the *arènes*, a stately amphitheatre where bull-fights, Provençal races and country dancing take place; a still impressive theatre; the *thermae* of Constantin; the renowned necropolis of the Alyscamps, an ancient cemetery where Dante came to meditate; the strange church of Saint-Honorat; Saint-Trophime, a splendid example of the « Roman-Provençal » style, which is flanked by one of the finest cloisters in the south of France... The heart of the city has yielded potteries dating from the VIth century B.C.; two former churches harbour innumerable statues, steles, capitals, and sarcophagi from local excavations. The Réattu museum has pieces of the past and the present in two contiguous XVth century buildings, and the Arlaten museum or « Palais du Félibrige » was created by Frédéric Mistral, who devoted to it his passion as well as the Nobel Prize money. A charmingly quaint place, it evokes the history, traditions, legends and crafts of Provence. It also shelters the most authentic cabin from Camargue.

Arles is the northernmost point of the melancholy marshy triangle formed by the two arms of the Rhône — a strange, paradox-

ical delta characterized both by water and by drought. If one wishes to discover the secrets of Camargue, one must leave the direct road from Arles to the Saintes-Maries-de-la-Mer, the road of the summer rush to the sea. The charm of Camargue is infinite under the fresh light of Spring or in the mists of Autumn, or monotonous when the soil crackles under the blaze of the noon sun in the dog-days; it is unexpectedly cut across by fences, canals, *roubines* (drains) and streams, and it must be explored with patience, preferably when the level light of dawn or sunset sharpens out the blurred outlines (a ten feet high mound looks like a hill!), colours the dormant waters of marshes and pools, and outlines the little black bulls and white horses gathered in *manades* under the watchful eye of nimble horsemen called *gardians*.

Camargue has kept its individual character in spite of the extension of the ricefields, of the developments in the Rhône valley, of the onslaughts of the sea and of the tourist invasion, wich jeopardize the fragile ecological balance of the marshy plain. It has pine, juniper and tamarisk as well as plants capable of resisting the biting effects of salt water: marsh samphire, salt-wort, water-purslane, red behen, rush and reed. If they can stand the agression of the *mangeance* (exasperating clouds of insects), tourists will see throngs of water-birds: hieratic flamingoes and

(following pages),

*Orange, the arch of triumph, built order to commemorate Caesar's tory over the people of Marsiglia, survived the vicissitudes of history (opposite).*

*Herds of white horses in semi-freedom can be seen in the wide expanses of secret Camargue where earth, water and sky are blended (just above).*

*Arles, the "Rome of Gaul", can boast of one of the masterpieces of the medieval provençal Romanesque architecture: the church of Saint-Trophime (bell-tower and cloister are shown in the lower right corner).*

*A landmark in the region of Aix, the Montagne Sainte-Victoire (following pages), a long chalk ridge scorched by the sun, was a favourite of Cézanne.*

herons, and flocks of migrator birds. This is a bird sanctuary, and efforts are being made to ensure that it shall remain unspoilt: a vast zoological and botanical reservation had been created even before World War II. Camargue has only one important town: Les Saintes-Maries-de-la-Mer, which is signaled from afar by the steeple of a suprising XIIth century fortified church which is the goal of the yearly pilgrimage of the *gitans.*

**From Massalia to the Europort.** Marseille is a complex metropolis where concrete looms up from the beds of the past; until recently, it was the "door to the East", and it is now the Mediterranean outlet of the European Common Market; it is still number one France's harbour. At the centre of a large suburbia, with traffic which is still congested in spite of the metro, and offering a mixture of Provençal picturesqueness and contemporary drabness, the huge city has a superb setting at the bottom of a deep bay surrounded by dazzling chalk mountains. The *préfecture* of Bouches-du-Rhône has kept its colourful and clogged Vieux-Port, which is practically in the same location as the *Lacydon,* the landing stage of ancient *Massalia.* The latter, founded in 600 B.C. by the Phocaeans, became the starting-point of the Hellenic influence over Gaul before coming under the rule of

the Romans with the creation of *Provincia romana,* the future Provence. The dock at the lower end of the famous Canebière — a wide, rather nondescript thoroughfare — is only used for small fishing craft and for the boats plying beween the city and the islands, particularly the Château d'If, an old fort used by Alexandre Dumas as a prison for his imaginary Count of Monte Cristo. The liners, the car-ferries serving Corsica, and the cargoboats moor in the Joliette docks, whereas the giant tankers use the huge docks of the southern Europort, stretching from the Gulf of Fos to Port-Saint-Louis-du-Rhône at the edge of Camargue.

The city is guarded by Notre-Dame-de-la-Garde, a XIXth century basilica with a steeple bearing a statue of the Virgin, the "Bonne Mère" of the Marseille people. Of particular interest are both sides of the Vieux Port, the narrow entrance of which is dominated by two forts: on one side of the dock is the basilica Saint-Victor and its "catacombs" — crypts dating in part from the Vth century —; the other offers the elegant XVIIth century townhall, the quaint Quartier du Panier, the former Hospice de la Charité, which was saved by a late renovation, the cold XIXth century cathedral, and the old romanesque church called "La Major". Marseille is rich with varied, intelligently organized museums; it also offers, to the west, the admirable Corniche, from which one can see the roadstead, the islands, and the mounts of Marseilleveyre.

Lovely, noble and secret Aix-en-Provence, although well connected with Paris by the motorway, belongs to quite another universe with its moss-grown fountains and its aristocratic townhouses. It is an endearing city, at once peaceful and lively, medieval in spots, predominantly XVIIth and XVIIIth century elsewhere; it is proud of its composite cathedral, of its townhall with its baroque front, and of its Granet museum; towering over it like a symbol is the Montagne Sainte-Victoire. This chalk mountain, the background to the Aix landscape, was indefatigably painted over and over again by Paul Cézanne, who was born and died there. Aix proved unable to keep his works, but it has attracted many other artists including Victor Vasarely, the pioneer of "op'art", whose foundation — an information and research centre conceived as a complement to the Gordes museum — is harboured in queer-looking hexagonal cells.

**Fjords and Dolce Vita.** The rocky coastline between the Marseille suburbs and Cassis, a lovely fishing harbour surrounded by hills grown with vines, olive-groves and orchards, is indented by ochre and

white *calanques* with musical names like Sormiou, Morgiou, En Vau, Port-Pin, which are still protected by their inaccessibility: it is easier to reach them by sea than by land, as the paths leading to them are vertiginous in parts.

Deeply notched by the sea, the *calanques* are overlooked by steep, barren walls and by desolate debris, then brighten up to pine-grown vales and to tiny beaches. Once threatened by a projected coast road against which the associations for the defence of the landscape were up in arms, they have retained their beauty and their mystery, and still provide nudists and solitary campers with many hidden nooks.

The jagged Provençal coast, hollowed out by creeks and coves, is heavily industrialized at La Ciotat (with dockyards for the building of the largest ships) and in Toulon, a long fortified harbour nestling in a moutain dent. Set in a roadstead and invaded by "blue collars" — the seamen of the French Mediterranean Fleet —, Toulon had to be rebuilt after World War II, when the finest French warships were scuttled in its docks. It retains its Provençal charm in the area around lovely Place Puget, and Mont Faron provides superb views over the ever lively sights offered by the roadstead. Though peaceful and populous in daytime, at night the "hot" streets lined with little bars crowded with provocative girls seem to be the « Pigalle » of Provence.

Near Hyères, the fine Giens peninsula looks to the Porquerolles islands with their quasi-tropical vegetation, to Port-Cros, fragrant with lavender and rosemary, and to the Levant islands, which are shared between nudists and the army. East of the twin towns of Saint-Raphaël and Fréjus (important Roman vestiges in the latter), the coast is dominated by the Maures Mountains, a world of its own, covered with a dark mantle of pines, cork-oaks, chestnut-trees as well as with prickly pears, agaves, eucalyptus and mimosas. In a wonderfully peaceful chestnut wood in the midst of the mountains (the elevation of which does not exceed 2,555 feet) can be found the Charterhouse of La Verne, a partially ruined fortified monastery.

Saint-Tropez (pronounced "Tropé") used to be a tiny fishing harbour and a little town full of salt and sunshine before the Belle Époque painters and Parisian high society fell in love with it, and Colette had a *mas, La Treille-Muscade,* accommodated for her. "The air is light, the sun wrinkles and dries the grapes ripening on the stocks, and garlic is great: what a country!" she wrote. "Indeed the invaders are building villas and garages and sham *mas* where they dance; indeed, the northern Barbar-

*The* calanques — *or small fjords — of Marseille, with their solitary creeks and steep cliffs, are paradise for those in search of quiet scenes or rock-climbing enthusiasts (opposite is the Calanque d'En Vau, near Cassis).*

*The spell-binding charm of Aix-en-Provence (opposite is the Pavillon Vendôme) is enhanced by aristocratic houses decorated with bossages, pilasters, and friezes as well as with fine wrought-iron balconies.*

108

ians are cutting up, speculating, deforesting. What a pity! "In the course of centuries, however, how many abductors have fallen in love with such a beautiful captive?"

The lovely little pink port was partially destroyed in 1944, but it was rebuilt with taste in the Provençal style before rising to fame again in the 1950's, when it was flocked with stars and starlets, beautiful girls and idle millionaires. Brigitte Bardot had to fence in her estate, *La Madrague,* in reedmats because it was besieged by photographers, and the nude-fans defied *Le Gendarme de Saint-Tropez* (the title of a film) when nude sun-bathing was still prohibited. Saint-Tropez became known all over the world as the capital of *dolce vita,* and its shady legend was responsible for its being flooded with Nosey Parkers more interested in seeing the stars than in admiring the paintings in the endearing Musée de l'Annonciade.

Today, celebrities are more discreet, and nobody is surprised at finding girls in the nude on the beach near the huge camping ground of Pampelone... The village is nonetheless crowded from July 15 to Sept-

ember 1, so that one should visit the tiny city with its fragrant pine woods and its lovely beaches in sleepy spring, autumn, or even winter.

**Côte d'Azur and Riviera.** Historians and geographers would be hard pushed to decide exactly where the Côte d'Azur begins: at Saint-Tropez? At Saint-Raphaël? Or at La Napoule? Poet Stephen Liégeard invented the phrase in the 1880's in order to distinguish between the French and the Italian Rivieras, but he was careful not to mark the boundaries of the enchanted coast in which the independent Principality of Monaco is inlaid. However, nobody in France is at a loss when one mentions « la Côte » without any further precision: within a few miles, it is assumed to include an ill-defined section of the Var coast, the shore of the Alpes-Maritimes, and the Monte-Carlo enclave.

The best and the worst can be found on the Côte d'Azur, which can be described as the touristic façade of Provence: concrete and old ochre-coloured stones including porphyry, pine forests and urban develop-

ments, peaceful nooks and human ant-hives, relatively active fishing harbours and the "new harbours" with moorings for yachts whose owners seem to never have heard about cruising. Sublime in places but totally disfigured in many others, as hope-

*Saint-Tropez, with a "miraculous" light playing on its colourful housefronts, and fishing-boats and yachts moored side by side in its harbour (above).*

*The celebrated Baie des Anges, along which stretches the city of Nice (top of page).*

and such shows as the Midem and the Festival du Cinéma fill the hotels during the low season. The setting is highly urban, of course, but once out of the traffic jams, one can rediscover the deep Provence by driving up to Mougins or to Grasse, a city with an old centre and the capital of the perfume industry. Beyond the Palm-Beach Hotel are Golfe-Juan, Juan-les-Pins and Antibes — a huge seaside complex out of which stands Cap-d'Antibes with its beautiful houses surrounded by evergreen lawns, pine woods, and luxury hotels.

Juan-les-Pins, a modern resort built without any planning, is almost characterless compared with Antibes (*Antipolis* under the Phoenicians): behind the sea-beaten walls is a picturesque district overlooked by the bright palace of the Grimaldis, and where are to be seen the findings of the excavations as well as the works of Picasso (who worked in Antibes and in Mougins before settling in Vence).

Nice is built on hillsides strewn with houses, while the ancient site of Cimiez spreads out behind the magnificent curve of the Promenade des Anglais and the pebble beach which hems in the Baie des Anges. There is now only one dense city between harbour and airport (the runways of which stretch out into the sea), but it has many facets. Nice, which used to be call-

lessly crowded in summertime as it can be endearing in the other seasons, the Côte d'Azur is a puzzle with a remarkable, probably even an incomparable, pattern. The warm sea, the pebble and sandy beaches where slender girls lie and roast, the Croisette and the Promenade des Anglais, the night and day hustle and bustle and the touristic facilities of all kinds attract a motley crowd of customers which, in summer, turns the Provençaux into a minority. The natural or artificial enticements of the "coast grill" somewhat outshine the treasures hidden in the hinterland dotted with villages set high up in the mountains, where it never occurs to you that the beaches are only a few miles away as the crow flies: the authentic Provence is still present behind Cannes, Nice, Menton and all the other resorts on the international sea-front.

In Cannes, the Croisette, a large seafront boulevard curving with some majesty between two harbours and overlooking beaches that have been sanded anew under the rows of mattresses and sunshades, serves as a runway to the hotels and to the Palais des Festivals. Below hillsides covered with houses and apartment buildings, the famous resort which was started by an English Chancellor, Lord Brougham, combines an old district with a distinct Provençal seal about it, called Le Suquet, streets dating from the Belle Époque, and innumerable modern buildings with all their balconies turned toward the sun. A many-faceted city as well as a seaside resort, Cannes attracts youngsters and old people, gamblers, wealthy customers of luxury hotels, yachtsmen, and simple visitors: a true holiday Babel!

Except in November and during the first three weeks of December, Cannes is always lively. Retired people crowd it in winter,

*Saint-Paul-de-Vence, a high village which is a favourite of poets and artists, consists in shady squares and little streets lined with pretty houses and made lively by bubbling fountains (opposite).*

ed the capital of the "French Riviera", is a crossroads made lively by trade and business, but with little industry. Although set within a fringe of suburbian concrete, it has not been submerged by it. The Place Masséna, which was laid out in 1835, has retained its Genoese character with ochre-coloured arches, and the old district stretching below the "Castle Rock", with its narrow streets, its high XVIIIth century houses and its flower market, is as picturesque as ever. The Italian character of old Nice, of Palais Lascaris and of several churches,

is due to the fact that the city was a possession of the Maison de Savoie until the 1860 plebiscite, which was followed by the reunion of France with the Comté de Nice (the present *département* of Alpes-Maritimes).

"A living goddess born out of a foamy sea with a kiss from the sun" (Theodore de Banville), Nice is a perfect starting-point for trips to the mountainous hinterland, which is overwhelmingly beautiful with its hidden villages and its old cities. One must tear oneself away from the *paseo* of

the Promenade des Anglais in order discover Cagnes, Saint-Paul-de-Vence wi its ring of walls and the Maeght Found tion, medieval Vence, the skiing stations Valberg, Auron, Isola 2000, the Turini pa Saint-Martin-Vésubie.

Beyond Nice is the sheer drop of t Alpes into the sea: the Corniches — hig roads offering viewpoints — give access La Turbie and to the Trophée des Alpes monument commemorating the Roman v tories), the dizzy eagle's nest of Ez and the medieval labyrinth of old Roqu

brune. Beyond the Monaco enclave, Menton is the last resort on the Côte d'Azur, near the Italian border: below the high wall of the mountain which protects it from the wind, it is a haven of warmth where lemon trees can bloom without fear of frost. Maupassant thought is was "the warmest, the healthiest of wintering towns". Menton has kept its colourful little harbour, its old houses and its enchanted gardens even while it had a modern harbour built. Twisty roads climb up to the villages set high up in the mountains: Italy is only a few miles away.

### The Principality of Monaco

*A sovereign monarchic state enclaved in a republic, the Principality of Monaco, situated on the steep slopes of the French Riviera, has become one of the world's capitals of gambling. Monte-Carlo is the name of its best-known district, where the casinos and the hollywoodian summer sporting clubs are. The city of luxurious hotels, of gambling, and of posh beaches, whose borders with France have* been open ever since 1865, is terribly short of space, so that property developers must build in height and encroach upon the sea. Picturesque old Monaco is located on the "Rock", between the prince's palace and the harbour fort. Overlooking it is the huge, austere Museum of Oceanography, with its wonderful aquariums. On the other side of the yacht dock, behind which the shopping district rises in tiers, is the gambling area to which Monte-Carlo owes its wealth; its most venerable building, the huge casino, was built at the end of the XIXth century by Charles Garnier, the architect of the Opera in Paris.

*Peillon* (below), *in the valley of the Paillon de l'Escarène, is one of the most picturesque villages set high up in the hinterland of Nice.*

# Corsica

**T**HERE CANNOT BE A DOUBT for Corsicans: their "mountain in the sea" is the most beautiful of all islands. They may be right: Corsica is smaller but more varied than either Sardinia or Sicily, and it offers gulfs, creeks and bays as well as valleys, plateaux and mountain-ranges. It stages a coupling of the sea with the sun, and in winter its mountains are capped with snow under a pure blue sky. It is covered with vines, with evergreen, impenetrable, fragrant *maquis*, with woods of olive-trees and forests of cork-oaks, pines, beeches, chestnuts, and high-mountain pastures. Every turning reveals a viewpoint (several panoramas are nothing short of sublime), and the narrow, winding roads run over passes, along torrents or by high lakes whose waters are still ice-cold even when the sea is warm.

Corsica is divided into two *départements*, but it seems to be composed of as many mini-regions as there are promontories and valleys. Do not get Ajaccio, Bonifacio and Bastia mixed up! Each Corsican belongs to his home town or village, to Cap Corse, to Nebbio, to the Balagne, to Asco, Valinco, the Sartène region or the Fiumorbo — but they all have a Corsican heart and are fluent in a language rooted in Latin though it sounds mostly Italian to the ears of the "continental" French people.

Corsican summers are hot and bright, but the island is most fragrant in springtime, when the extremely varied flora blooms precociously: "I would know it by its fragrance", said Napoléon, who was the greatest Corsican with Pascal Paoli, even though their destinies were quite different: whereas the former became the Emperor of the French, the latter fought for the independence of the island and wrote a short-lived constitution for it. The coast, which is beautiful almost everywhere, is rocky and jagged except in the east, where it slopes down into endless beaches. Saint-Florent, L'Île-Rousse, Calvi, Porto, Cargèse,

Ajaccio, Propriano, Solenzara, Porto-Vecchio and many other seaside resorts attract the summer crowds while the admirable Corsican mountains remain almost deserted.

There is no architectural wealth to match the beauty of the natural sites in Corsica, even though there are many Romanesque chapels and a few classical and baroque churches, citadels and fortifications, and fine villages often set high up in the mountains and no less often nearly deserted. And yet the population refuse to sell their strongly-built houses. Corsica is an island where everything must be seen, without looking for the ideal route and without being afraid of monotony: it simply does not exist.

### Historical landmarks

*Corsica, often torn by wars, tumult, and upheavals, has miraculously retained its idiosyncrasy in spite of it having been either conquered or ruled, at least in part, by Rome, by the Pope, by Pisa, Genoa, Aragon, England, and France. Napoleon's native island was declared French in 1789 by the Assemblée nationale in spite of the resistance of the men of Pascal Paoli. After being only one* département *for a long time, in 1975 it became two: Haute-Corse (Bastia), Corse-du-Sud (Ajaccio). In recent years a variety of regionalist, autonomist, and even independentist movements have aroused agitation.*

*The Corsican village of Vescovato (opposite), which rises in tiers up a hill overlooking the fertile Casinca plain, seems to have been spared by the tourists' invasion.*

*In the Corsican coastline — a rocky lacework washed by the transparent waters of the sea — one can find both the appeals of lovely shores and* of a spell-binding hinterland (above, the old city of Bonifacio).

*Set high up on a rocky promontory in the middle of a mountain cirque, the narrow houses of the old city of Corte (following pages) are huddled at the foot of the citadel.*

# Burgundy

**B**URGUNDY IS THE COUNTRY of castles, of Romanesque churches, and of great wines, but it also has ploughed land, stock farming, and some industry (Le Creusot). An important thoroughfare, Burgundy is patterned by the upper valley of the Seine and its tributaries in the north, and by the Saône in the south. Once the homeland of the Eduans, who sided with Vercingétorix without undue enthusiasm, Burgundy was a kingdom under the Burgundians, then the best part of a larger state reaching up to the North Sea — only to be broken up by Louis XI when he shrewdly got the better of Charles le Téméraire. As a present-day administrative region, it covers four *départements*: Yonne, Nièvre, Côte-d'Or and Saône-et-Loire, which still correspond approximately with the land owned quite independently by the Grands Ducs d'Occident from the end of the XIVth to the end of the XVth century. The dukedom had been granted as an apanage to Philippe le Hardi by his father Jean le Bon in 1364, but the Dukes tended to forget its royal origin: they never stopped increasing it through marriages and legacies. Indeed, the architectural wealth and idiosyncracies of Burgundy bear witness to the fact that it was once more than a province. One of the most French and of the least autonomist regions of France, Burgundy still boasts of its "Grand Siècle", the glory of which adds up to such prestigious heirlooms as Cluny and Cîteaux.

**A Museum in a Palace.** The past is present everywhere in the rather well-circumscribed limits of the centre of Dijon, whose historical heart it has been possible to preserve and to renovate in the very midst of expansion. Even while it became a small metropolis with a modern periphery, the city of wines, of mustard, and of gingerbread has managed to keep its old housefronts without flanking them with concrete; now cleaned and restored, they have a charming pedestrian area as a centre. The fine city whose many steeples were counted with wonder by François I, boasts of its cathedral, its churches, its huge ducal palace with its remarkable museum, its aristocratic townhouses and its venerable, pot-bellied houses. A late comer in history, it soon ousted Autun and

Beaune, flourished under the Grands Ducs, and was the affluent seat of a Parliament during the XVIIth and the XVIIIth centuries. The tokens of the end of the Ancien Régime are particularly remarkable: the palace was decorated according to the tastes of the Grand Siècle, and by the side of the picturesque medieval houses the members of Parliament had sober, elegant dwelling-places built as signs of their social rise.

The historical part of Dijon is not even the size of an *arrondissement* in Paris, and yet there is a surprise in store with each step taken in it. It has two poles not far from each other: the Saint-Bénigne cathedral, keeping watch over an old abbey and over a district full of churches; the Palais des Ducs, a huge and motley building in the vicinity of which the tiniest street conceals architectural curiosities. The old district, which was surrounded in the XIXth century by wealthy buildings, seems to be miles away from the new suburbs and from the nautical entertainments of Lake Kir, which is not far from the ruins of the Charter-house of Champmol: only a doorway and the famous "Well of Moses", both sculpted

by Claus Sluter around 1400, are still to be seen.

The cathedral, a large, austere Gothic nave dating from the XIIIth and XIVth centuries, conceals the surprising, half-buried vestiges of an old Romanesque church: excavations have revealed a strange rotunda dating back to 1001, a shadowy labyrinth, and the bottom of a sarcophagus in which may have lain the body of legendary Saint Bénigne. Nearby are vestiges of an important abbey, the huge Gothic dormitory and massive Romanesque rooms of which now harbour the collections of a fascinating archaeological museum showing very fine medieval sculptures as well as mysterious, Gallo-Roman ex-votos unearthed at the source of the Seine (which used to be considered as a god). In the vicinity of Saint-Bénigne and in the midst of the old district are to be seen two secularized churches: Saint-Philibert, robust and harmonious, and Saint-Jean, where Jacques Bénigne Bossuet, the future "Eagle of Meaux", was baptized.

The Palace of the Dukes of Burgundy, which became a "royal dwelling", then a townhall, used to have a Holy Chapel full of a wealth of riches — but it was torn down in the XIXth century. In its place is now the wing, harbouring the main rooms of an eclectic Museum of Fine Arts which, with the addition of the former arms room, is both a smaller Louvre and a museum of modern art (where two huge tombs can be seen, and the admirable threefold altarpieces saved from the disgraceful destruction of the charterhouse of Champmol). The palace, which was endlessly renovated and enlarged by the Dukes, was metamorphosed during the XVIIth and XVIIIth centuries when it took on a new look under the direction of Hardouin-Mansart, and later of Jacques Gabriel. Now a vast, cold edifice, it is patterned around three courtyards and dominated by the old tower of Philippe le Bon; it incorporates several vestiges of the Middle Ages, among which the spectacular kitchens of the Dukes.

The main courtyard of the palace opens up on the harmonious arcades of Place de la Libération, formerly Place Royale. This vast architectural unit is situated in the very centre of the older Dijon, in the middle of picturesque, narrow streets lined with

*Left is shown the none too felicitous (according to some) reconstitution by Viollet-le-Duc of the tympanum on the central doorway of Vézelay, with its minutely detailed Christ in majesty.*

*"Moses' Well", by Claus Sluter, a masterpiece of medieval sculpture, is one of the very few vestiges of the Champmol charterhouse, once the burying-place of the dukes of Burgundy (opposite).*

timber-framed houses of medieval burgesses and with luxurious townhouses of members of Parliament and of the legal professions: the streets called Chouette, Vannerie, Verrerie, belong to quite another time. From busy Rue Musette can be seen the surprisingly light façade of Notre-Dame, a jewel of the XIIIth century and the dwelling-place of the Jacquemart family, whose "father" — an automaton from the belfry of Courtrai — was given to Dijon by Philippe le Hardi, and whose other members, a wife and children, were later built in order to help him strike the hours. Saint-Michel, a Gothic church, has a Renaissance, almost a mannered façade. The former Saint-Etienne cathedral is the seat of the Chamber of Commerce; it also houses the Rude Museum (numerous copies of the works of the great Dijon-born sculptor).

**From the vineyards of Chablis to the forests of Morvan.** Tourists coming from the north reach Burgundy in the region of Joigny, an old city on the banks of the slow, winding river Yonne (one can get a fine view of it from the Côte Saint-Jacques). Auxerre (to be pronounced "Ausserre") is also watered by the lovely Morvan-born river; the best view of the old city is from the right bank when it is tinged by the setting sun. Its his-

torical heart is overlooked by Saint-Etienne, a Gothic cathedral with an ornate, dissymetric façade (one of the towers was left unfinished) and remarkable door-

ways. The composite former abbey-church of Saint-Germain, which was built apart from its Burgundian-Romanesque belltower, was raised on the very spot where the great bishop was buried. Beneath the cold upper church is to be found a labyrinth, a dimly-lit crypt, most of which date from the IXth century.

Auxerre has retained a small vineyard, the property of a hospital, which produces

a wine made famous by Alexandre Dumas in his *Dictionary of Cooking*. Although the Yonne region is still for the most part a wine-growing region, particularly with Chablis, it also has many orchards, which are beautiful in springtime, when the cherry-trees are in blossom.

The acropolis of Vézelay, clinging to a high promontory surrounded by walls, used to be a meeting place for pilgrims on their

way to Compostelle, and for crusaders ready to fight for the Holy Places. On top of the "inspired hill", the luminous Sainte-Madeleine basilica, which was saved from total ruin by Viollet-le-Duc, is now a touristic landmark. The building of La Madeleine began in 1120 after a former church had burned down. It opens on a huge, superb Romanesque narthex in which the inner central tympanum stands out as one of the masterpieces of Burgundian art. The nave, in which white and brown stones alternate in a breathtaking perspective, is decorated with famous storiated capitals. The flock of old houses and the defences of Vézelay are outlined against the foothills of Morvan, a massif of hills covered with dark forests interspersed with compensating lakes and enlivened by streams. This enclaved region is now opening up to tourism, with the equipment of its stretches of water, especially the Lac des Settons.

Morvan, a region with both vast panoramas and hidden paths, has several "doors" of access: either Saint-Père (with a fine Gothic church), Avallon, an old city poised on a spur, Saulieu, a gastronomic stop ever since the XVIIth century, or Château-Chinon with its unrestricted outlook.

**The Glories of Yore.** Lower Burgundy includes Puisaye (Colette's home country: there she was born and spent her childhood, as told in *La Maison de Claudine*) and part of Nivernais. It stretches far east of the A6 motorway, to the borders of Champagne and to the crossroads of Lan-

*At Vézelay, the storiated capitals of the Romanesque nave illustrate many scenes from the Bible and from the lives of the saints (opposite, the mystical mill) with both fantasy and realism.*

*Vézelay* (above), *set on top of a hill overlooking the valley of the Cure, was a pilgrimage centre and a start-* *ing-place for one of the itineraries to Saint-Jacques-de-Compostelle.*

122

gres (whose bishops ruled over Dijon for a while). With gentle valleys and wind-blown plateaux, it is a region of castles, abbeys, old stones and many interesting sights. Tonnerre, which is built on the slopes of a hill, was martyred during World War II; however, it has kept both its old hospital (with a prodigious timberwork) and the Renaissance house where the mysterious Chevalier d'Eon was born. In the vicinity are two of Burgundy's most interesting castles: Taulay, which is full of charm, and Ancy-le-Franc, a huge, austere square behind the walls of which is a wonderful Renaissance courtyard.

At the edge of a large forest, near the inexhaustible rustic sources of the Douix, Châtillon-sur-Seine lies between the arms of the whimsical river. Overlooking the city is the early Romanesque church of Saint-Vorles, which was partially destroyed

in 1940. It was a miracle, however, if fire spared the lovely Renaissance house sheltering the archaeological museum and the matchless treasures dug out in 1953 on Mont Lassois, near the village of Vix. Specialists from all over the world marvelled at the size and weight (457 pounds) of a huge bronze vase, the largest crater from Antiquity. Decorated with gorgons and with a frieze of chariots and warriors, it was laid in the tomb of a princess around 500 B.C. It was probably cast by Greek bronze-makers who had settled in Italy, thus showing evidence of the old commercial relations between the Mediterranean and the Celt areas.

Set high up in the hills and surrounded by massive walls, the medieval city of Semur, with its narrow streets and its superb church, keeps watch over Auxois, a region of isolated mounds and fertile val-

leys which provides a transition between the mountains of Morvan and the chalk plateaux of Burgundy. Near the important railway station of Laumes stands one of the most famous hills in France, on which are the old village of Alise-Sainte-Reine and the Gallo-Roman excavations of Alésia. Mont Auxois itself serves as a plinth for the monumental statue of Vercingétorix, complete with beard and moustache. The leader of the Gaul uprisal against the Romans was besieged by Caesar's ten legions and forced to surrender in 52 B.C. From this date a new era began.

The Auxois region is strewn with old towns and villages, with castles like Epoisses and Bussy-Rabutin. The latter, set in a background of greenery, has nothing spectacular in terms of architecture, but it is one of Burgundy's unusual sights. Exiled by Louis XIV for having shown disrespect to the king, Roger de Bussy-Rabutin used his own walls in order to project his obsessions, his vanity and his aggressiveness: he directed a crowd of painters to portray the best-known among his contemporaries, to paint bizarre symbolical scenes, and to picture a frivolous marchioness upon whom the author of *L'Histoire amoureuse des Gaules* wished to wreak his vengeance.

The river Seine springs up near the beautiful road from Auxois to Dijon; it is only a rivulet babbling in the tall grass at the bottom of a cool vale.

**Hillsides and vineyards.** South of Dijon can be seen the first vines, clinging to the steep cliff of a massif (la "Montagne") indented with *combes*: this is the "Côte de Nuits" to which are attached such famous names as Gevrey-Chambertin, Chambolle-Musigny, Vougeot, Vosne-Romanée, Nuits-Saint-Georges, etc. Shared as it is between dozens of owners (the Burgundy vineyards are quite parcelled out), the renowned "climat" (the local name for a vineyard) of the

### Historical landmarks

*Burgundy, where Vercingétorix was defeated by Caesar in 52 B.C., got its name from the Burgunds, a Germanic people which established a first kingdom there in the Vth century. After many divisions and reunions, Burgundy was attached to the French Crown in the XIth century. Robert le Pieux gave it to his eldest son, who left it to his younger brother, Robert. The latter thus became the first of twelve Capetian dukes, whose line came to an end in 1361. The duchy then fell back to the Crown, and it was almost immediately given as his fief to Philippe le Hardi, the first of the Grand Dukes of Occident. After inheriting Flanders and Artois, he bequeathed a vast state to his son, Jean le Bon, whose successor, Philippe le Bon, was one of the greatest sovereigns in European history.*
*Charles le Téméraire (1433-1477) endeavoured to transform the duchy of Burgundy into a kingdom, to the detriment of the French Crown. However, he fell a victim to both his own ambitions and the craftiness of Louis XI, and he failed. After his death, the duchy was definitively joined to France.*

*A jewel of the Renaissance and a home of Protestantism during the Wars of Religion, the castle of Tanlay (opposite) is surrounded with wide moats peopled with swans.*

*Burgundy (above, Semur-en-Auxois) has kept many vestiges of the troubled Middle Ages, a time when its lords would protect themselves behind strong walls.*

Clos de Vougeot stretches from the castle to the vast Romanesque storeroom and to the huge "cuverie" (vat room) which is the meeting place of the Chevaliers du Tastevin and their guests.

Whereas the hillsides of Nuits yield great red wines — with very few whites —, the Beaune ones, more pleasant-looking, have both reds and whites. To the north and to the south-west of the ramparts of Beaune, they offer gentle, varied landscapes which are particularly beautiful at the Combe de Pernand and in the vicinity of Savigny. The finest places are to be seen as one follows the winding roads between the drystone walls: Aloxe-Corton; Pernand-Vergelesses; Savigny-lès-Beaune (with a beautiful XIth century belltower); Pomard, a big village with strong houses; Volnay; Auxey-Duresses; Meursault with its Gothic spire; Puligny- and Chassagne-Montrachet; Santenay, a wine-growing town and a spa (it owns two hot springs, but it is probably better known for its wines and casino).

Running parallel to the "côtes", the "hautes côtes" or upper hillsides, with their cool, picturesque landscapes, are also covered with vineyards. In the south are yet other vineyards, those of the hills of Chalon, of Mercurey, of Gevrey. Vineyards also cling to the heights in the regions of Cluny and Mâcon: the pouilly-fuissé vinestocks spread beneath the high rock of Solutré, a natural keep under which an important pre-historic site was discovered. At this point, one has almost reached Beaujolais — another wine-growing region.

Between Côte de Nuits and Côte de Beaune is Beaune, an old city hemmed in by ramparts. A busy wine-trading centre and the capital of Burgundy as far as famous wines are concerned, it is a small city out of a cherished past. Wine-merchants, whose signs can be seen everywhere, have taken over the bastions and turned the medieval cellars into huge wine storerooms. Beaune is somewhat jealous of Dijon, which was favoured by the Dukes. However, it owns a star monument, the Hôtel-Dieu, and two jewels — the Notre-Dame collegiate church and the Dukes' house — as well as many fine townhouses, churches, and deconsecrated convents.

With its shining, many-coloured tiles, the superb Hôtel-Dieu is bound to be a surprise to whoever is ignorant of the Flemish past of Burgundy. The decorative pattern of this almshouse recalls the heyday of Flanders, over which the Grands Ducs ruled. It was built by Chancellor Nicolas Rolin in the XVth century, and served as a hospital until 1791. Its extraordinary ward, with its chestnut framework, ends with a chapel; the kitchens and dispensary have kept their old-time aspect. The place is also a museum with tapestries, furniture, and above all the renowned triptych of *The Last Judgment*, a masterpiece painted by Van der Weyden in the middle of the XVth century.

Behind its XIVth century porch, Notre-Dame reveals a medley of architectural styles; it has frescoes dating back to the 1470's, and the five remarkable tapestries telling the story of *The Life of the Virgin* (c. 1500). The former Hôtel des Ducs became a "royal dwelling" after the death of Charles le Téméraire; it now harbours a museum of Burgundy wines which is remarkably well laid out, but which focuses on the past more than on the present.

**A Romanesque Cézanne.** Built on a panoramic height aside from the main north-south thoroughfare and a dozen miles away from Mont Beuvray on which the Eduans built their fortified capital named Bibracte, Autun is an old city with many vestiges of its Gallo-Roman heyday. It is overlooked by a harmonious sanctuary of considerable size, the Saint-Lazare cathedral. Although its exterior aspect was modified, its interior has retained its Romanesque aspect, including a stupendous collection of high capitals telling a wealth of episodes from the Scriptures. A large porch protects the doorway with an extraordinarily beautiful tympanum sculpted in the 1130's by a stonecutter whose name has not remained anonymous: Gislebertus, or the "Romanesque Cézanne" according to André Malraux. Under the watchful eye of a hieratic Christ, a crowd of lively high-relief characters illustrate several phases of Doomsday.

Near the cathedral, the Rolin museum is the gathering place of collections of works of art from all periods. Among its treasures are a glamorous *Eve* by Gislebertus taken from the cathedral, the remnants of the tomb of Saint Lazare, a very fine *Nativity* by the Maître de Moulins, and the charming Autun *Virgin*. Along with those in Dijon and in Châtillon, this museum is one of the most interesting museums in Burgundy.

South of Autun, beyond the industrial landscapes of Le Creusot and Montceau-les-Mines, Charolais offers its green pastures and Brionnais its countryside dotted with Romanesque churches. The centre of the cult of the Sacred Heart and a beautiful old city, Paray-le-Monial owns a superb basilica built out of white stones in 1109. Mirrored in the Bourbince, a quiet little river, it looks like the perfect example of the Cluny architectural style. Behind it, the Parc des Chapelains is periodically opened to thousands of pilgrims: the cult of the Sacred Heart of Jesus was advocated in the XVIIth century by a visionary nun from Paray-le-Monial, Marguerite-Marie Alacoque, who was canonized in 1864.

**The Saône as a link.** The Seine springs up north of Dijon only to swerve away from Burgundy; but a beautiful river from the Vosges mountains, the Saône, winds through the Dijon region before becoming the main river of upper Burgundy, when it runs parallel with the main thoroughfares (N6 and A6). It seems to slow down along the embankments of the old Chalon and in Tournus, where two arcaded towers signal Saint-Philibert, a former Romanesque abbey-church whose rough, powerful narthex is in contrast with its slender, pink-hued nave. The river goes on flirting with a region of soft hills whose hazy or hoary landscapes were sung by Lamartine. A beautiful Regency house in Mâcon, his native town, has been turned into a museum.

The poet's memory lingers on everywhere in the neighbourhood. He tended the vines of the castle of Monceau even while he wrote

*Ever since the XVth century, the Hôtel-Dieu at Beaune (above) has nursed the sick and fed the poor with the money got each year from the sale of the prestigious wines of the Hospices de Beaune.*

his *Histoire des Girondins*, and he immortalized Bussières in his *Jocelyn*, "disguising" the old castle of Saint-Point in the romantic-Gothic fashion. "The obscure village of Milly" — now Milly-Lamartine, the goal of a pilgrimage — inspired him with one of his most famous *Méditations*. Even though born in Mâcon, he pretended he had been born in this charming village where he spent his childhood in a wealthy house, and where he played with the farmers' children.

The steep rock of Solutré, which overlooks rows and rows of chardonnay vine-plants, can serve as the boundary of both Lamartine's country south-west of Mâcon, and of historical Burgundy. The silvery Saône runs at the foot of the heights of Beaujolais, which could be called the wine-growing suburbs of Lyon. Across from it, on the left bank, Bresse spreads out its softly rolling hills, which were belatedly joined to the Dukedom of Burgundy. In this region of big farms, some of which have kept their old "saracen" chimneys — curious miniature-minarets —, ever since the Middle Ages people have been devoted to the breeding of poultry; the "bressan" chickens, with their white feathers, are now submitted to the strict regulations of an "appellation d'origine contrôlée". However, Bresse also owns a jewel: the flamboyant church of Brou, in the periphery of Bourg-en-Bresse; its choir shelters splendid stalls and extraordinary monumental tombs which are masterpieces of the XVIth century.

Apparently an extension of Bresse, the flat watery region of La Dombes is strewn with shallow, ill-shaped pools which are periodically stocked with fish, then emptied for tilling, to be used as pools again. La Dombes, however, is not only a huge fish-preserve and grazing land. It is also a stop fo migratory birds. With its vast water expanses and its aviary, the exemplary ornithological park is more than a bird-zoo: it is a sanctuary sought by birds of all kinds: greenfinches and song-thrushes, finches and colverts.

**The Roundness of Beaujolais.** Everything is pleasantly rounded in Beaujolais: the hills are softly rolling, the roads are winding, and the wine-growers, with their sturdy common sense, are open, easy-going fellows. Officially, the Beaujolais wines have a right to be called burgundies, even though they are the produce of a particular stock called gamay; historically, however, the former fief of the lords of Beaujeu was quite distinct from the dukedom, and remained independent from it until it was joined to the crown of France. One leaves Burgundy as one leaves Mâcon.

*After her beloved husband's death, Marguerite d'Autriche, Duchess of Savoie, had a church built at Brou, where her own tomb is in the purest flamboyant Gothic style (opposite).*

Beaujolais has big, wealthy villages and strong houses covered with Roman tiles, but no remarkable monument. However, it unrolls gentle landscapes, a hundred belvederes, green vineyards, and golden stones with warm, luminous hues. In the rear of the wine-growing area there is also a country of pines and broom, with hills covered with grass. This is "La Montagne", and it is quite beautiful even though tourists are more drawn by the wine villages: Saint-Amour, Juliénas, Chénas, Fleurie, Chiroubles, Villié-Morgon, and by sunny Mont

Brouilly, on top of which is a chapel called Notre-Dame-du-Raisin.

Wine cellars and stores, where one drinks cup after cup as one expresses one's satisfaction by dropping a judicious «y goûte ben» from time to time, are as many stops on the whimsical itinerary of the wines road. Upper Beaujolais — the land of "crus" and "villages" —, with its steep hillsides, is covered with vines dressed in a way which is special to the region. Now essentially a wine-growing country, it has been thriving ever since the beaujolais

boom: the international reputation of this little fruity wine which must be drunk when it is still "green" is relatively recent. To the south, lower Beaujolais is still dedicated to mixed gardening. However, it produces "simple" kinds of beaujolais which local people rather sornfully call "bastard" wines.

Villefranche-sur-Saône, which was founded by the lords of Beaujeu to whom it owed its franchise, is set in a rather nondescript surburban belt. Its very old houses and its "traboules" (passageways between two streets) vie with those in Lyon, which is the pole of attraction for the little wine capital.

# *the Lyon Region*

**A**N IMPORTANT CROSSROADS CENTRE at the confluence of the Saône and the Rhône, and a metropolis in terms of the Common Market, Lyon is both bimillenary and ultracontemporary. The tower shooting up from the futuristic district of La Part-Dieu makes a pair with the unusual basilica built in the XIXth century on top of a hill encrusted with Gallo-Roman stones; the Romanesque church of Saint-Martin d'Ainay stands near the commuting centre or Perrache, a thick layer of concrete hiding the Second Empire architecture of the railway station. The heart of a conurbation of some 1,150,000 inhabitants, and (with Saint-Etienne and Grenoble) one of the three heads of the Rhône-Alpes region, Lyon has been a bold innovator and an ambitious planner even though it is still under the spell of its long past.

The Roman-Byzantine basilica of Notre-Dame-de-Fourvière and the large Roman vestiges stand above a matchless Renaissance district, the older Lyon of rue Saint-Jean, with its *traboules,* its slender turrets and its elaborate staircases. This area, which used to be dingy, has now recovered its appeal with its Tuscan charm and its arcaded courtyards linked together through long corridors which enable one to pass (« trabouler », from the Latin *transambulare*) from one street to another. This resuscitated district is dominated by the Saint-Jean cathedral, the primatial of the Gauls, the construction of which was begun in the XIIth century; its rather austere façade stands over a foundation of marble slabs torn from Trajan's forum (the name of Fourvière is derived from *Forum vetus*); it was used for two Councils as well as for

*Autun — Augustodunum for the Romans —, of which it was said that it was both "the sister and the rival of Rome", spreads around its stately romanesque cathedral and watches over Morvan (opposite).*

the wedding of Henry IV and Catherine de Médicis.

Above the peninsula formed by the Saône and the Rhône, the plateau of La Croix-Rousse stands apart with its impressive *traboules;* it has kept the mark of the Amphitheatre of the Three Gauls, and retained the high houses where the *canuts* or silk-weavers would work their noisy looms patterned by Jacquard and called *bistan-claques.* Although it stands apart, La Croix-Rousse is as intimately associated with Lyon as Montmartre is with Paris: "In other places, people are descended from the crusaders; in Lyon, one is descended from La Croix-Rousse..." As to the wealthy bourgeois peninsula, it is given space by the vast Place Bellecour, and animation by the pedestrian streets under which runs the metro; and it has kept its admirable townhall, its monumental Trade Centre, and its Stock Exchange, a stately symbol of busy Lyon.

**The Eastward Thrust.** Lyon was born in 43 B.C. upon the heights of Fourvière; then the city went down to the Saône, and incorporated the peninsula and the slopes of La Croix-Rousse. Only at the end of the XIXth century, with the laying-out of the Brotteaux and of La Guillotière and the setting-up of the big industries, did the city cross over the Rhône. Ever since then, it has kept spreading eastward, until it practically merges with Villeurbanne (the seat of the Théâtre national populaire). The left bank of the Rhône has been metamorphosed by the construction of "a town within the town", the huge, modern area called La Part-Dieu, a spectacular reunion of administrative buildings, commercial offices, shopping centre, auditorium, cultural centre and covered market-place (a large, traditional market for wholesale and retail set in a contemporary setting).

Lyon is a disconcerting, inexhaustible city with a deep attachment for its own peculiarities. It is commercial and industrial, and yet it has always been a lively intellectual centre, devoted to art and culture, with young, enthusiastic audiences. It is proud of its opera-house, of its theatres, of its bold auditorium. The city where Rabelais had both *Pantagruel* and *Gargantua* printed, boasts of more than twenty museums, some of which are still relatively unknown even though they are remarkable. One of the most original museums in Lyon, the historical museum of Woven Materials, is located in an elegant XVIIIth century townhouse next to the interesting Museum of Decorative Arts: on display are embroideries of all periods, flamboyant silk fabrics, modern compositions, all kinds of interplay between threads and colours... And in the Historical Museum in a fine house of the older Lyon Guignol, a true "gone" (a child of Lyon), presides over a meeting of puppets.

The peninsula also harbours rich museums: the Museum of Fine Arts, set in a former monastery as big as a palace, and the twin Museums of Printing and Banking, both in a fine XVIth century house. A surprising and fine concrete building, the remarkable Museum of Gallo-Roman Civilization, stands out on top of Fourvière in front of the ruins of ancient *Lugdunum:* its wide windows open on the vast excavation grounds where the remnants of the theatre founded by Augustus and of an odeon are particularly noteworthy. The original ramps of this highly logical and practical museum allow one to discover a thousand statues and artifacts as well as the famous "Claudian table" which was found in a vineyard in the XVIth century. It has the text of a speech in which Emperor Claudius, who was born in Lugdunum, asked the Senate to grant the Gauls eligibility to Roman magistracies. This — the past in a modern setting — is a good symbol of Lyon.

# the Rhône Valley

**A** CORRIDOR FOR THE *MISTRAL* and the main way of access to the *Midi,* the Rhône valley is a natural boundary between the Massif central and the Alps. It widens and narrows, and gradually takes on the colours of Provence. Like the Loire and the Garonne, the powerful river, which is cut across by dams, is lined with vineyards: the Côtes du Rhône vineyards stretch on both banks, often on terraces dug out of the steep hills, from Ampuis (côte-rôtie) down to Châteauneuf-du-Pape and Tavel. The Condrieu region yields the white and fragrant viognier as well as the rare château-grillet; between Tain, Tournon and Valence are the «hermitages», red or golden white: saint-joseph, cornas or saint-péray. The vineyards are balanced with orchards, which are sometimes associated with market-gardening: peach-, apricot- and cherry-trees have taken over the Rhodanian piedmont.

A city of artistic and historical interest, Vienne is Roman with the harmonious temple of Augustus and Livia, Romanesque with the church and cloister of Saint-André-le-Bas, and Gothic with the Saint-Maurice cathedral. Part of the treasures yielded by the soil, in particular some admirable mosaics, are on show in one of the oldest churches in France, Saint-Pierre. At the crossroads of Vivarais, Vercors and Provence, Valence has grown into a large city — unfortunately separated from the Rhône by the motorway. Modern buildings and boulevards hem in the old city with the monument of the Pendentif, the Romanesque cathedral, and the bishopric now turned into a museum (with a remarkable collection of paintings by Hubert Robert). To the south, Montélimar, the city of *nougat,* has grown on the edge of Tricastin, a small region grown with hollyoaks, olive-trees and pines, and strewn with castles. There is the true geographical beginning of Provence...

*Following a deliberate plan, many of the fine housefronts in old Lyon have been restored to their former state (opposite, the Tour rose in the Rue du Bœuf; in it is a corkscrew staircase).*

*Halfway between Burgundy and Provence, Vienne has many monuments which bear witness to the part played in the Antiquity; it also has a finely decorated Gothic cathedral (opposite).*

# Massif central

**N**EAR CONDRIEU, whose charming little harbour recalls Saint-Tropez, the massif of the Mont Pilat is the separation-mark between the Rhône valley and the Loire basin. Its rounded ridges and its eroded granite rocks are the foothills of the Massif central, a large hercynian bas-

tion enclaved in the heart of France. Although industrialized in and around Clermont-Ferrand, it is mostly rural and traditional with its "black lands", many orchards in its valleys, and rich meadows for its cattle. In Auvergne, where grass if often covered with snow during the winter months, are volcanoes, either relatively recent cones or time-worn *puys*.

Massif central is a land of spas (Vichy, Châtelguyon, La Bourboule, Le Mont-Dore, Royat), the slopes of which are used for cross-country skiing and sometimes downhill skiing too; and it offers a splendid variety of natural places of interest (panoramas, running waters, churches, medieval eagle's nests). Le Puy is built on the slopes of a high rock in a hollow bristling with volcanic peaks. In the midst of old houses where a few lace-makers are still at work, picturesque Rue des Tables winds its way up to a Romanesque masterpiece showing a Byzantine influence: the strange cathedral of Notre-Dame, which one reaches by walking up a 102-step stairway, used to be a stop for pilgrims on their way to Compostelle. On the high altar is a famous Black Virgin which replaces another, burnt under the Revolution. North of the marian city, a slender peak of lava is the foundation of the Romanesque chapel of Saint-Michel d'Aiguilhe, which was also influenced by eastern art.

*In the heart of Auvergne, Salers, the seat of a judicial court in the XVth century, has kept many old houses built in lava by the well-to-do bourgeois of yore (top).*

*The Danse macabre (above, on the left), painted in tempera on the walls of the north aisle of the choir in the celebrated Chaise-Dieu abbey — an authentic masterpiece of ogival archi-*

*tecture —, is a remarkable illustration of the haunting presence of death in medieval art.*

*A beautiful example of auvergnat Romanesque architecture is given by the church of Saint-Nectaire (above), a village set on Mont Cornadore in the middle of a wooded scenery.*

In Saint-Austremoine at Issoire, an impressive Romanesque sanctuary (above), the choir, richly decorated with paintings and sculptures, sets off the strong, severe appearance of the church.

The basilica of Notre-Dame-du-Port (above), whose oldest part dates from the XIth and XIIth centuries, was the historical core around which Clermont-Ferrand was built.

Set on top of a volcanic hill, the castle of Busséol (following pages), now restored, overlooks the wide expanses of Limagne.

# the Alps

**F**ACING THE POWERFUL SLOPES of the Massif Central, the fore-Alps are the eastern limit of the Rhodanian corridor: Vienne belongs to lower Dauphiné, Valence is near Vercors. The latter, with its deep forests and its vast meadows, is a chalk fortress hollowed out by gorges, whose belvederes overlook Grenoble and the Graisivaudan wedged in between the Chartreuse massif and the ridge or Belledonne. The Alps, an enormous mass topped with eternal snow, a formidable welter of massifs and valleys, of pointed peaks and uneven plateaux, seem to be an impassable barrier at the southeastern borders of France. However, they are not a rampart, especially as they are cut across by a network of thoroughfares which have been used ever since the Antiquity. There are high, enclaved valleys such as beautiful

Queyras "where cocks peck at the stars", mountains reserved for chamois and climbers, and frozen deserts — but the Alps have long been humanized and strewn with cities some of which are important, and with innumerable villages.

The French Alps, shaped by torrents and glaciers, are quite varied — wet in the north, dry and much less green in the south. They have been divided into three regions by history: Savoie, which was belatedly joined to France; Dauphiné; and Haute-Provence. The two Savoie *départements* and part of Dauphiné are included in the powerful Rhône-Alpes region in which Grenoble, a booming city with a first-rate location, matches the influence of Lyon. In the midst of an ordinary modern setting, Chambéry, the former capital of the Dukes of Savoie, has retained a network of myst-

erious passageways and old streets watched over by a much-remodelled castle. Aix-les-Bains is a big, rather nondescript spa in a first-rate location, where the poet Lamartine tried to cure his "mal du siècle"; he courted Madame Charles on the banks of the Lac du Bourget in which the abbey of Hautecombe is mirrored. On the bank of another lake is pretty Annecy, with its theatrical setting. Thonon and Evian are spas on the banks of Franco-Swiss Lake Léman.

**In the country of white gold.** At the foot of the gigantic mass of Mont Blanc and of Aiguille du Midi — a fabulous belvedere from which the Mer de Glace runs down — is a little city without much architectural charm: Chamonix, the capital of mountain-climbing and a big skiing centre. Quite near Switzerland and connected with Italian Val d'Aoste through a road-tunnel, "Cham" is busy in all seasons as it attracts tourists and climbers from all over the world. One must use the cable-cars in order to reach the skiing slopes, because, like Megève, Saint-Gervais and Morzine, Chamonix is not high enough to make skiing possible all year around. The local

*Annecy owes its being called "the Venice of Savoie" to its canals and bridges. An island in the Thiou river, the strange Palais de l'Isle —*

*formerly a prison, a courthouse, and even a mint — still keeps watch over the old town (above).*

*The Mer de Glace (Sea of Ice, opposite), shown here from the Aiguille du Moine, is a frozen torrent "running" down from Mont-Blanc over a distance of four miles.*

people, who knew nothing of winter sports, used to prefer the shelter of valleys, so that there are very few old villages high up in the mountains: Val d'Isère, Bonneval-sur-Arc, Molines-en-Queyras are exceptions.

After the valley villages had been equipped with spiderwebs of cable-car lines, the "white gold boom" caused modern ski centres to be built, sometimes in concrete hidden behind a veneer of wood, as high as 6,000 to 6,500 feet, on formerly deserted slopes where snow is guaranteed. L'Alpe d'Huez, les Deux-Alpes and Chamrousse

were among the first. Courchevel has become a model, with its network of tracks laid out rationally and linked with Méribel, Belleville and Val-Thorens.

Technocrats and promoters now speak of "third-generation ski-villages". This is a deliberately functional universe where everything is geared to skiing, where towers and buildings replace the old *chalets:* Avoriaz, Flaine, La Plagne, Les Arcs, Tignes, Le Corbier, Pra-Loup enable one to put on one's skis practically in front of one's door.

### Historical landmarks

*Dauphiné long belonged to completely independent princes whose family name (or nickname), dauphin, remains a mystery. In 1349, one of these princes, heirless, gave up his land to France. Dauphiné was an apanage for the eldest sons of kings, who all held the title of Dauphin until their accession to the throne. Savoie, a rival and often an adversary of Dauphiné, was a large independent state whose counts and, later, dukes also controled Piedmont, Sardinia, and the area of Nice. It remained separate until 1860, when most of its inhabitants voted to be incorporated to France.*

# Franche-Comté

EAST OF BURGUNDY, on the left bank of the Saône, rugged Jura stretches like a crescent, touching Lake Léman and reaching as far as the Alps. While part of it belongs to Switzerland, the French Jura takes up most of Franche-Comté (*Comté*, which refers to the County of Burgundy as opposed to the Dukedom, used to be feminine). The summits of the Jura are not very high, but the whole ridge, covered as it is with large pine forests, has a definite mountain-like aspect, with its steep slopes, its deep *cluses* (caved-in passages between two valleys), and its spectacular *reculées* (huge recesses notched in the mountain).

Winters are long and cold: a thick layer of snow clings to the soil for several months, so that skiing is possible in several places. The homely resort of Les Rousses, which shares its skiing tracks with Switzerland, does not offer alpine slopes, but it always has lots of snow. The climate explains why the roofs are so large and so strong, and why the south- and east-oriented walls are covered with scales of wood or of sheet-iron. Springs are full of flowers, and summers are quite dazzling; even though the *chaux* (chalk slopes) remain dry, almost desert-like, the green foliage of both meadows and *joux* (woods of beeches and firs) blossoms out under a blue sky mirrored in dozens of lakes.

The Jura of the *fruitières* (milk-farms) and of the *comté* (a cheese akin to *gruyère*) extends into the plateaux of Haute-Saône in a transition between Burgundy and Lorraine. Besançon, a city huddled under a high rock in a bend of the Doubs, has kept the aspect of an old stronghold with the citadel built by Vauban, and the remnants of its ramparts. It has a severe beauty of its own. Ever since the end of the XVIIIth century, it has been a centre for clock- and watch-making, and about a hundred years ago, the industry of artificial silk or rayon was born there.

Between the foothills of Jura and Bresse is a rolling country of vineyards and orchards called Le Vignoble, where the wines of Château-Châlon, Arbois and L'Etoile are produced. East of Dole and of the forest of Chaux, the salt-works of Jura were the reason behind the building of an unusual industrial lay-out in the XVIIIth century. Claude Nicolas Ledoux, an architect bursting with imagination though rigorous and obsessed with social preoccupations, planned an "ideal city" under the form of a circle, which was a revolution in the art of city-planning. Unfortunately, he could never finish it. The existing buildings were abandoned in 1890 when the exploitation of rock-salt began to collapse. The former royal salt-work of Arc-et-Senans was saved from ruin *in extremis*, however; it is now a centre for the researchers of the Ledoux Foundation and in summertime it harbours artistic performances.

*Lods (opposite) is a quiet, pleasant village on the banks of the Loue, a river running down from an impressive cirque of rocks through a series of waterfalls down to Mouthier-Saint-Pierre, after which it calms down.*

*A thousand windings river, the Doubs traces out a sinuous and picturesque valley through the Jura's plateaux. Here it will flow, deeply embanked between narrow gorges, there it will form a still waters expanse.*

*The royal saltworks of Arc-et-Senans was built under Louis XVI as the heart of an ideal city which was never built. It was planned in a circle at the centre of which stood the administrative building (opposite).*

# Alsace

ALSACE CONSISTS IN TWO *DÉPARTE-MENTS,* Haut-Rhin and Bas-Rhin, which are so tightly bound together as to form a separate world which Germany bitterly fought over and failed to assimilate... It is sedate and original, and it has a quiet beauty of its own. From north to south are to be found three cities and a series of wealthy villages whose names are often ended with either a "heim" or a "willer". Alsace is one of the most easily circumscribed provinces in France, and it is both very particular and very French in spite of its Germanic dialect and of its Rhenish aspect. It has practically no fallow land and no uninhabited places, and it has always practised mixed farming intensively, which accounts for its pleasant rural landscape: orchards, tobacco- and hopfields, woods, and vineyards unroll between the Vosgian heights, the Rhine valley and the northern and southern forests.

It is a homely, hearty, gracious province, with a high degree of tolerance (churches and temples are often side by side); it has tended to the crual wounds of three wars, and forgotten the dark times of annexation. As in Switzerland, its towns and villages are trimmed and primmed with great nicety, and they often display romantic towers, ruined *burgs,* and innumerable half-timbered houses with high gables framed in by ample roofs with turned-up edges. Alsatians are well-to-do and they show it without ostentation; they often dress with flowers their fine, wealthy, more bourgeois than aristocratic houses.

Of course there are housing estates and rows of electric pylons in Alsace, but the sites are well protected and the old districts, with their harmonious white or pink housefronts, are lovingly enhanced. The way in which the old streets of Strasbourg and Colmar and those of such beautiful villages as Equisheim have been renovated is exemplary. Local costumes and the big black knot worn by women now belong to folklore, and the storks have often deserted their nests (although efforts are being made to reacclimatize them). The image of the province, however, is still quite typical, and this is not entirely due to the innumerable pots of geraniums, to the timber-framed houses, to the *winstubs* where only wine can be drunk, or to the *caveaux* (cellars) with a congenial atmosphere. Alsatians do not look like Erckmann-Chatrian's famous *Ami Fritz,* yet they are deeply attached to all that goes into the making of the incomparable charm of the "neatest" of the regions of France.

A long, bright clearing in contrast with the dark line of the Black Forest across the river Rhine, Alsace is a juxtaposition of several little regions welded together as entities which history rather than geography can explain. From Strasbourg, which is connected with Germany by the Pont de l'Europe, to Mulhouse, near Bâle and Switzerland, *via* Colmar, there is no clear-

*Whereas on the peaks of the Vosges mountains stand age-old citadels built during the tumultuous feudal times (opposite is shown the impressive, red sandstone fortress of Haut-Kœnigsbourg), in the villages on the "wine road" traditional festivities are held each year at harvest time (above).*

cut division. Landscapes change only gradually from Wissembourg in the north (where Stanislas Leszczyński and his daughter Marie, the future queen of France, lived) to the spur of Ferrette in the south. The chestnut- and fir-covered valleys originating in the Vosges mountains — the "hautes chaumes" — are isolated from one another, but they open up on the plain between hills covered with vineyards: each low town controls its own valley, or valleys.

**A collapsed massif.** Alsace owes its aspect, its growth and its architecture to man, but its structure and its unity are derived from a formidable geological upheaval: the collapse of an old massif between the Vosges and the Black Forest. For the most part, it is made of a long plain overlooked by picturesque hills leaning against the Vosgian block, whose bald summits, worn round by erosion, stand out from the forests. The presence of many kinds of soil explains the difference in vegetation and the variety of farms. The plain is either covered with rocks out of which oaks grow, or with a rich silt called loess; it is marshy in the Ried, which is green and wet even though drainage has partially changed its aspect. The sunny hillocks below the Vosges at the upper end of the valleys are covered with vines which are trimmed high and whose yield is the best in France. The riesling, traminer, gewurztraminer, tokay, pinot, and sylvaner vine-plants cling to sometimes quite steep slopes and run down to villages as clean as new pins.

The wines — Alsace's big business, especially in the Colmar region — do not bear the name of a château or of a famous brand, but only that of the plant they are made from: a riesling, a tokay... In order to distinguish between the best bottles and the rest, one must be attentive to the label and cognisant of the names of the owners and traders who are the aristocracy in a field which is broken up into many small units. The only exceptions are zwicker and edelzwicker, which are blended wines, "little whites" to be drunk at the counter and which leave no memory even though they quench one's thirst.

Alsatian beer is also renowned, although it vies with the highly characteristic white wines only in the north, where the main breweries are.

**Three Cities and a hundred Villages.** Three cities of unequal importance stand out from the tight network of towns and villages surrounded by meticulously tilled lands. Strasbourg, a large, lively city between the branches of the Ill, a river harbour and a border crossroads, is bourgeois with its fine houses dressed with flowers, princely with its stately Château des Rohan and its noble townhouses, but also industrial and hard-working. It was fashioned during the XVth and again during the XVIIIth centuries — though it has kept fine vestiges of the XIVth century — and wedded with water; it is highly picturesque in its old districts, particularly that of the "petite France", but it is not a postcard city, frozen in the past: modern life puts up with old stones. It is the seat of the Council of Europe; it harbours a great European fair each year in september; it is an intellectual and economical metropolis where Gutenberg invented printing: Strasbourg is characterized by a perfect balance between past and present.

*In Alsace, life in the villages depends very much on the vineyards covering the sunny hillsides (opposite). Strasbourg, the metropolis, has been able to adapt to modern times without relinquishing its glorious past (on top, the cathedral, a beautiful legacy from the Gothic age).*

The surprising, openwork spire of the Gothic cathedral, one of the most original in France, stands high above an old district which was restored with taste and turned into a pedestrian area. The large nave, whose pink sandstone is getting darker every year, is dressed with stupendous stone lacework and lit up by the shimmering mosaic of precious stained-glass windows dating from the XIIth, XIIIth, and XIVth centuries. Each day, the hour of 12:30 is struck by an astronomical clock peopled with automatons. Nearby, in front of the old Alsatian houses of the Quai des Bateliers, the Ill mirrors the façade of the harmonious Château des Rohan, whose luxurious drawing-rooms and basement house the rich collections of three museums. The Alsatian Museum, which has been set in a fine XVIIth century house across from the former Customhouse, enables one to travel in a past which is still near and deeply endearing.

Colmar is a middle-sized city with an intense charm about it. It owns a famous museum (Unterlinden, with Issenheim's altarpiece), but one might go as far as saying that the whole city is but one museum: renovation, conducted in the best possible way, has resuscitated the old "Quartier des Tanneurs", the "little Venice" the gables of which are mirrored in the Lauch. From Unterlinden to the former boatsmen's houses, it is one pageant of Alsatian houses, churches, and the old custom house. Not far are the Vosges mountains and the wine-growing villages: Equisheim in its ramparts, watched over by three towers; Kaysersberg, stretching at the opening of a deep valley; Riquewihr, a surprisingly theatrical village whose long main street is always crowded with tourists; Ribeauvillé in the north, with its traditional Fête des Ménétriers (strolling fiddlers).

Mulhouse, the big city of the south, has fine houses and a townhall dating from the Rhine Renaissance. It has retained a definite industrial calling as the former continental "Manchester". A free city once part of the Décapole — a confederation of Alsatian towns —, it kept its own independence when the treaties of Westphalia joined Alsace to France. Only in 1798, by a deliberate vote, did Mulhouse join France. In the XVIIIth and XIXth centuries, prosperity came from the manufacture of printed cloths. The "printed cottons" form Mulhouse, which originally were meant to imitate the prints imported from the East,

had an incredible success. The Museum of calico printing owns millions of such prints, which bear witness to the inexhaustible imagination of the cartoonists.

West of Mulhouse, on the road to the Bussang pass and to the panoramic Route des Crêtes, in Thann stands the slender, elegant church of Saint-Thiébaut, a former Gothic collegial church locally called a "cathedral" and often dubbed Alsace's Sainte-Chapelle. South of Mulhouse, Alsace ends with a very individualized region: the hilly Sundgau is a blending of forests, orchards, and crops around Altkirch, the high little capital of the region; strewn with lakes and quite green, it has a pronounced Swiss character.

by the presence of beeches; it also has chestnut-groves on the Alsatian side, out of which are made the props used by winegrowers. The forest is still under exploitation, but tractors have replaced the *schlittes* (sledges loaded with logs sliding on a log road and held with great difficulty by lumbermen taking their stand on the cross-pieces). Beginning at a height of 3,300 feet, the forest, which was used by the violin-makers, by the iron-masters, and by the glass-cutters, gives way to the "hautes chaumes" — low-grass slopes with tufts of bilberries. The "marcaires" — the shepherds of the past — used to stay in the mountains from May to October; there they would make the Munster, a cheese which is

now manufactured in the valleys. Their rough houses, the "marcaireries", are now in ruins or transformed into inns for cross-country skiers and summer hikers.

The river Moselle separates into two branches at Epinal. The latter, which is built in the woods between mountain and plain, was made famous by naive illustrations called "images d'Epinal". Whereas the east side of the Vosges has wines, the west side has mineral waters, with the spas of Plombières-les-Bains, Bains-les-Bains, Contrexéville et Vittel. In the latter two, which are pleasant resorts with casinos, parks, and many trips to be taken in the neighbourhood, millions of bottles are filled, corked, and labelled each year.

# Vosges

HE VOSGES MOUNTAINS, a big massif with thick reliefs out of which stand rounded tops called *ballons,* present a steep side to Alsace and a gentle slope to the Lorraine plateau. A rampart for dry Alsace, they occasionally gets lots of snow, which allows some downhill but mostly cross-country skiing. The broad, squat farms with thick walls and large roofs are adapted to a tough climate. The mountains, worn down by glaciers, are strewn with charming lakes in isolated amphitheatres or in valleys blocked by moraines; one of the finest — and the largest — is Lake Gérardmer, in the centre of a crown of wooded slopes. Whether granite or sandstone (red sandstone was used for building churches and castles), the Vosges look like "true mountains" almost everywhere even though the highest *ballon* (Guebwiller) is only 4,671-feet high. The summits, passes, and pretty Route des Crêtes provide ample panoramas, while the higher valleys are steeped in solitude and silence, only troubled in summer by the tinkling of cattle-bells.

The large Vosgian forest is thick and stately; it is dark with slender spruce-firs, lighter with pectinated pines, made brighter

*Colmar is the most typical of Alsatian cities, with its narrow streets and its wonderful half-timbered housses. The preceding pages show the famous Rue des Marchands.*

# Lorraine

ORRAINE IS QUITE APART from Alsace, and yet its limits are vague, as it gradually merges into Meuse, Champagne and Franche-Comté. It was the homeland of Jeanne d'Arc, who was born in Domrémy in 1412: there she heard the holy voices urging her to free France from the English. The region which the Germans intended to incorporate covers four *départements:* Moselle, Meurthe-et-Moselle, Meuse, and Vosges. With its cold winters and hot summers, the Lorraine plateau looks austere with its large fields and its meadows without a hedge or a tree,

## Historical landmarks

*IIIrd century: first Germanic invasions.*
*End of VIth century: Clovis seized the regions of Meuse and Moselle.*
*IXth century: Treaty of Verdun. The future Lorraine fell under Lothar I's rule and became Lotharingia, then passed to Louis the German.*
*End of Xth century: Lorraine was divided into Haute and Basse-Lorraine.*
*XIIth-XIIIth centuries: the cities became independent.*
*XVIth century: France occupied the three bishoprics of Metz, Toul and Verdun.*
*XVIIIth century: the duchy of Lorraine was ceded to Stanislas Leszczyński, Louis XV's father-in-law and the dispossessed king of Poland.*
*1766: death of Stanislas. The duchy went back to France.*
*1871: Germany annexed part of Lorraine.*
*1918: France recovered the lost territory.*
*1940-44: German occupation and de facto annexation.*
*End of 1944: the Liberation.*

and with its villages strung along main streets, whose house-fronts are indented by wide doorways (houses are built in depth, giving on to invisible gardens at the back). The wine-growing region of Moselle (where vineyards have recently been giving way to fruit-trees, however) is softer, more pleasant, and brighter (from the colour of the rocks): it has been nicknamed "smiling Lorraine".

An extension of the coal-field of the Saar, the coal-mining region stretches away from the German frontier at Faulquemont, on both sides of the East motorway. To the coking-plants and the steam-generating stations of the coal country correspond the huge steel-works of the iron country at Longwy, Thionville and Briey. At night, with the chimneys standing above the forest and hiding away the industrial landscape, it is a flamboyant, impressive sight. Ever since prehistory, salt has been extracted from the Nancy region. Along with the coal fields and the iron-works, the salt deposits make up the famous lorrainese "triangle".

**The Horrors of War.** Lorraine, all too often a war-torn area because of its geographical situation, was sorely tried during World War I. Today Verdun — where the crucial treaty of 843 was signed in order to parcel out the legacy of Charlemagne — is a quiet *sous-préfecture*. However, the city of the Côtes des Meuses (not far from the Argonne) cannot forget the Great War: being a strategic place, it was totally devastated when the armistice was signed. The monu-

without a kingdom and the last Duke of Lorraine. Under the rule of this Polish prince of the *Erklärung,* Nancy was metamorphosed: the old medieval city and the new, XVIth century town were united. He had the walls torn down in 1750, and he gave the city the most perfect architectural development of the time: the Place Stanislas, with its elegant lodges, its splendid gold-fitted gates, its fountains, and the Place de la Carrière, which opens up on a colonnaded oval courtyard. The former Duke's Palace, the long, austere façade of which is decorated with the Porterie, a flamboyant and Renaissance masterpiece, harbours the important Historical Museum of Lorraine (superb collection of copper engravings by Jacques Callot). The XVIIIth century also left its mark on religious architecture, particularly with the church of Notre-Dame-de-Bon-Secours.

Metz, the other large lorrainese city, the "city with the twenty-two bridges", has a fine location at the confluence of the Seille and of the Moselle rivers. This pleasant city is no less than a monumental museum, with its noble Place d'Armes, its classical town-hall, the Place Saint-Louis and its arcades, the medieval Porte des Allemands, and the churches. Saint-Etienne, the cathedral, a Gothic masterpiece with wonderful stained-glass windows, looks perfectly homogeneous; and yet it consists in two churches at a right angle. The highest tower (288 feet) which is used as a belfry, harbours an enormous tenor bell, "Dame Mutte", weighing 11 tons.

ment to Victory, the Fort de Vaux nearby, and the huge ossuary at Douaumont bear witness to the incessant fighting and above all to the massacres of 1916, when more than 400,000 French soldiers died in order to "hold" Verdun.

North-east of Lorraine, the Meuse winds along in the Ardennes mountains, which seem to have kept alive the memory of the four legendary Aymon brothers who, according to a *chanson de geste,* rode Bayard, the fabulous horse. The Ardennes, which also stretch over Belgium, are only 1,653-feet high at the highest point, but their surface is quite rugged and their climate is rough: they look like real mountains. The area was also sorely tried in 1914-1918 and again in 1939-1940. It is covered with a

fine, deep forest of dark oaks and pale birches, and in the mysterious undergrowth of ferns, innumerable wild boars roam about. Charleville, Rimbaud's hometown, which is now associated with the twin city of Mézières, is centered on harmonious Place Ducale, with XVIIIth century arcades evocative of Place des Vosges in Paris.

**Nancy's fine vistas.** The wooded hill in which Maurice Barrès saw his "colline inspirée" at Sion-Vaudémont is a belvedere overlooking southern Lorraine between Meuse and Moselle, two pretty rivers enframing the major part of the natural regional park. A tributary of the Moselle, the Meurthe waters Nancy, the former capital of Stanislas Leszczyński, a king

*The core of Nancy, one of the finest cities built during the XVIIIth century, is Place Stanislas (above), which was designed by Héré and decorated with beautiful wrought-iron gates by Lamour, and with fountains by Guibal (opposite).*

149

# Champagne

CHAMPAGNE CANNOT BE REDUCED to a vineyard, even though the latter is known all over the world. Between the Seine and the Marne, the chalky Champagne, which used to be called "pouilleuse" (dingy) because of its naturally poor soil, stretches north of Troyes, a city of art rich in half-timbered houses and in Gothic and Renaissance churches. It used to be the capital of the County of Champagne, and Bernini compared it with a little Rome. It has lost several of its former sanctuaries, yet it still bristles with many steeples. The Saint-Pierre-et-Saint-Paul cathedral, the construction of which lasted from the XIIIth to the XVIth century, has kept its shimmering windows, among which the famous stained-glass called *The Mystical Wine-Press* (1625). Troyes, whose Museum of Fine Arts houses remarkable collections of paintings and sculptures, is an important crossroads in the vicinity of Burgundy. The surrounding countryside has become fer-

*"As the bubbles of this wine sparkle / So does the wit of Frenchmen dazzle". Thus did Voltaire define the nectar produced by the celebrated Champagne vineyards (opposite), which spread around Reims, the city of kings and one of the landmarks of Christian architecture (above, the Smiling Angel on the cathedral front).*

tile thanks to technological improvements in agriculture: the white chalk stretches, darkened in patches by pine woods, are now covered with fields of cereals and beetroot. Farmers still raise pigs in order to make their famous chitterling sausages.

To the south-east lies another Champagne, wet and green and pleasant, dotted with quiet hamlets and big, timber-framed farmhouses; it stretches its rolling hills and its woods between the chalk region and

### Historical landmarks

*451: Aetius, the Roman general, defeated Attila's Huns, on the Catalaunian fields, between Châlons-sur-Marne and Troyes.*
*486: Clovis seized Champagne.*
*496: he was baptized at Reims, which thus became the cradle of the Franc monarchy.*
*IXth century: Norman invasions.*
*Xth century: Hungarian invasions; the county of Troyes fell by inheritance to the Vermandois family, which joined it to the county of Meaux.*
*XII-XIIIth centuries: the counts of Champagne were among the most powerful lords in France; large fairs brought wealth to the cities.*
*XIVth century: Champagne was united to the French Crown.*
*XVth century: Joan of Arc crowned Charles VII at Reims.*
*End of XVIIth century: Champagne was invented, a wine whose creation was attributed to don Pérignon, a Benedictine monk.*
*1814: the battles over Champagne caused the fall of the Empire.*
*1915-18: the battles over Champagne played an important part in the First World War.*

the Barrois (the Bar-le-Duc region). It also has large, dense forests, one of which, called Forêt d'Orient, has been turned into a natural regional park (its lake is used as a stop by migratory water birds). In the church of Chaource, a big village twenty miles away from Troyes, is a superb *Mise au tombeau* dating from the XVIth century. However, the village is probably better known for its unctuous cheese.

**The Champagne of champagne.** East of chalky Champagne and of Sézanne, on the slopes of long, rolling hills topped with little woods, are the orderly rows of vine-plants: this is the Côte champenoise, the summit of which (Montagne de Reims) does not even reach 900 feet. This is the country of the merry-making wine.

Champagne exports its strong, heavy bottles by millions of dozens, the total yearly production sometimes being over 150 millions. At the end of the XVIIth century Dom Pérignon, a monk of the abbey of Hautvillers, is reported to have invented the process by which is manufactured the matchless "bubble-wine". The process is used in other regions and in other countries, but only a Champagne champagne is a true, great champagne.

Stretching over the *départements* of Marne, Aube, and Aisne, the vineyards, which wind along the slopes of the chalky hillsides, are practically all either pinot noir or chardonnay blanc (the latter bearing some resemblance with the Côte des Blancs south of Epernay). After being "manipulated", the wine ages in endless galleries and huge rooms dug into the chalk and kept at a constant temperature. These *caves* or cellars, sometimes as big as cathedrals, are often opened to visitors.

Originally a "quiet" wine (only too ready to bubble up naturally), champagne won over a privileged minority when, in the XVIIIth century, it was systematically turned into a sparkling wine. It is now being exported in more than 150 countries, and its prestige has never diminished in spite of ruthless competition. It is produced by wine-growers called «récoltants-manipulants», who manufacture their own wine, or by cooperatives, or yet by companies with famous names who buy their grapes and sometimes even own their vineyards: Krug, which boasts of a very small production; Roederer, whose range has always been narrow; Bollinger; Mumm, a company founded in 1734; Veuve Clicquot-Ponsardin (there really was a widow!); Moet et Chandon, the biggest of all, quoted at the Stock

Exchange; Perrier-Joët, Lanson, Pol Roger and many others whose beginnings date back to before the Revolution. Most of the large champagne firms have their headquarters in Reims or in Epernay, the two capitals of champagne wine.

**The coronation cathedral.** Reims, a large and beautiful city even in the Gallo-Roman period (during which many of the chalk-pits were dug; they now serve as cellars), stands on a subsoil tapped with galleries where millions of bottles are ageing. The city with hundreds of posters for champagne traders belongs with the history of France: in 496, Saint Remi baptized Clovis there, and most of the kings were crowned there too. Notre-Dame, a sublime Gothic cathedral where the Maid took Charles VII for his anointment, stands in the middle of the city with its sumptuously sculpted façade on which can be seen statues including the famous *Visitation* group and the no less famous angel called *The Smile of Reims.* The sanctuary, the style of which is as pure as can be and is best admired at the fall of day, nearly vanished during the Great War, when it was both bombed and burnt; next to it, the archbishop's palace was totally destroyed. The remarkable Saint-Remi basilica, a former abbey church, had to be restored too.

Epernay, the other capital of the wine of merry-making, is on the bank of the Marne. A middle-sized city without architectural riches, it has an interesting Museum of Champagne Wines. Under the hillsides is a thirty-mile labyrinth of galleries and cellars. The touristic road of the Côte des Blancs takes the visitor to Vertus, a big, old village with a spring at the chevet of the medieval church.

*From vinestock to bottle, many — and all delicate — are the phases in the making of the sparkling champagne (top left, the "remueur", one in charge of slightly turning the bottles during months in a row).*

*Patience and craftsmanship were needed to restore Notre-Dame-de-Reims to the unmatchable purity of its style (opposite, the West façade). From the time when it was the cathedral of coronations remains the chalice of Saint Remi (above, XIIth century).*

# Picardie

IN THE NORTH OF THE PARIS BASIN is the rich plateau of Picardie and it's valleys, a region of intensive farming and market-gardening, with a coast edged with sand-dunes and lined with seaside resorts. In the pale gold sand and under the green shelter of its pines is the largest of them, created during the Belle Époque and crowded each summer with people from the North of France and from Paris: le Touquet-Paris-Plage. Called the pearl of the Côte d'Opale, this international resort is linked by an endless beach with Berck, where bone diseases are cured. North of this, with the exception of the Somme and of the Canche estuaries, the coast runs up in a straight line to Boulogne-sur-Mer, France's number-one fishing harbour; then it rises in cliffs at Cape Gris-Nez, which is the threshold of Pas-de-Calais; it becomes Flemish at Calais, industrial in Dunkerque; next is Belgium.

Quiet Picardie was a land of frequent invasions and was bitterly fought over

*In the middle of a long ribbon of sand running along the Channel, Picardie opens up into a wide estuary which is deserted by the sea at low tide: it is the bay of the Somme (above, with the "sauterelliers" of Le Hourdel). Before reaching the sea, the lazy Somme flows through Amiens, the capital of Picardie, which boasts of the largest cathedral in France (opposite).*

Notre-Dame d'Amiens, which was built without interruption in the XIIIth century, and in which Viollet-le-Duc saw a true "stone Bible", is the largest, the most harmonious, and the most homogeneous of the great Gothic sanctuaries in France. In order to decorate it, the medieval sculptors vied with each other in talent. Above: *the Golden Virgin, on the doorway of the southern arm of the transept.* Opposite: *the beautiful God of Amiens, on the central door mullion.*

by England, France, and the Dukedom of Burgundy. There were many Gallo-Roman farms on this green land on which many battles took place; it was nonetheless the cradle of Gothic art, and it can boast of many monuments. Amiens, its peaceful capital, where the Somme river branches off into several arms, is proud of its immense and pale Notre-Dame cathedral, a "stone Bible" with admirable sculptures, and a masterpiece of balance and harmony. Almost white at the break of day, dun at noon, and pink in the evening, this XIIIth century sanctuary was "the ogival church *par excellence*" for Viollet-le-Duc. It is the largest Gothic cathedral in France, although it would have been passed by Saint-Pierre in Beauvais... if it had been completed. Abbeville, a sea-harbour on the Somme, the estuary of which attracts water-fowl, has lost its claim to the picturesque with the ruin wrought during World War II, but it has miraculously kept the façade of the Saint-Vulfran church, a jewel of flamboyant Gothic style.

Often compared with Normandy as well as with Switzerland, Thiérache, with its running streams and its green valleys, is a cattle-raising country with big, pleasant farms where milking cows graze (ever since the Middle Ages, a square strong cheese, the maroille, has been made there). Laon, a true acropolis, has an exceptional location on top of a rocky belvedere. Both robust and light, the towers of its cathedral stand above the ramparts and the old streets of the high city, which used to be the capital of Carolingian France and became an archbishopric.

### Historical landmarks

*Gallo-Roman period: Picardie, already rich and flourishing, was joined to Belgium by the Romans.*
*Middle Ages: a powerful feudal system, often ecclesiastic (abbeys), governed the region.*
*XIIth century: Flemish immigrants imported the textile industry, which made the bourgeois in the cities quite wealthy.*
*XII-XIVth centuries: French kings progressively incorporated Picardie.*
*Hundred Years' War: England endeavoured to conquer Picardie and gave the cities of the Somme to the Duke of Burgundy.*
*1482: the Treaty of Arras; Maximilien gave up Picardie to Louis XI.*
*XVI-XVIIth centuries: Spanish invasions.*
*1814: French campaign, ended by Napoleon's abdication.*
*1914-18: French and English offensives.*
*1939-40: campaign of France and battle of the Somme.*

# *Flanders*

**T**HE OLD FIEF OF THE DUKES of Burgundy, now divided between France and Belgium, is both an industrial and a rural land. Between the hills of Artois and the plateaux of Hainaut and Cambrésis are plains with a heavy soil, rolling hills, and spoil-heaps under an immense, often grey sky. This flat country whose low coastline was partly won over the sea and developed into polders, is divided into wet, green landscapes and the factories of the coalfields and of an industrial complex dedicated to textiles. The coal-mining area, which is less and less active, has been called the "black country". How different are the austere, monotonous, dark-brick mining towns from the rural villages, where comfortable houses are turned away from the street, and again from the large farms somewhat like strongholds! Flanders are a puzzle to Mediterraneans — and yet it is far less monotonous, and above all more gracious than one thinks; the Flemish people are realists who conceal a hearty temperament under an apparent coldness; they have kept a sense of entertainment and have held on to their merry *kermesses*.

**Belfried Cities.** The capital of French Flanders, Lille has long passed the brick walls which used to circumscribe the city. General de Gaulle's native town, where many

### Historical landmarks

*Gallo-Roman period: the region was part of the province of Belgium II.*
*IVth century: Franc and Saxon incursions.*
*Vth century: the area was ravaged by the Salians, then germanized by the Ripuarians.*
*VI-VIIth centuries: the abbeys promoted the textile manufactures.*
*IXth century: Norman incursions.*
*Xth century: establishment of the County of Flanders.*
*XIIth century: economic growth and creation of powerful merchant associations. Philippe Auguste reinforced the royal suzerainty.*
*XIVth century: textile slump caused skirmishes between cities; Flanders incorporated into the duchy of Burgundy.*
*XVth century: Habsburg domination.*
*XVIth century: Charles Quint broke the last ties of vassalage between France and Flanders.*
*XVIIth century: France slowly recovered French Flanders.*
*1815: Battle of Waterloo, and Napoleon's downfall.*
*XIX-XXth centuries: during the wars of 1870-71, 1914-18, and 1939-44, Flanders was the theatre of many battles.*

monuments of the XVIIth and XVIIIth centuries are still to be seen, forms an enormous industrial metropolis with Roubaix, Tourcoing, and other towns united into one vast conurbation. An active city with a tendency to noctambulism made even younger by its university, it is most lively in the area of the Grand-Place (Place du Général-de-Gaulle), of the old, baroque Stock Exchange, and of Alignement du Beau Regard — a series of venerable town-houses dating from the XVIIth century. Since the middle of the XIXth century, Lille has been deprived of a communal tower — a shocking anomaly in the country of belfries. In the 1930's, a belfry was built under the form of a brick-

and-concrete skyscraper, a 344-feet high giant at the top of which one discovers an immense panorama. The Museum of Fine Arts is one of the richest in France; it owns important collections of early masters as well as paintings of the Flemish, Dutch, and French schools.

Arras, the capital of Artois, which boasts of a superb group of Flemish buildings; Cambrai, the capital of Cambrésis, one of whose archbishops was Fénelon; and Valenciennes, the modern capital of Hainaut, have managed to retain their autonomy in spite of the huge Lille-Roubaix-Tourcoing conurbation. Cambrai, which is overlooked by a spectacular, 230-feet high

belfry, lives by the time struck by Martin and Martine, the two Jacks of the townhall clock; it still manufactures "bêtises" (mint-candies). Valenciennes, on the banks of the Escaut, was severely damaged by the wars; today, hosiery factories adjoin steel-plants and chemical industries: almost nothing is left of the graceful lacework which used to be the city's glory.

Maubeuge has developed on the Sambre, which merges into the Meuse in nearby Belgium. Here, too, is an industrial landscape which suffered in World War II. Once fortified by Vauban (it was a powerful stronghold), the city gets livelier in July with the Beer Festival.

A flat threshold where invaders marched past through the centuries, the Vermandois region has ill-defined borders and stretches its regular fields around Saint-Quentin, a martyr-city of World War I, and rises in tiers up a chalk hill hollowed out by galleries and cellars. Watching over the channelled Somme and the Isle pond, the city can legitimately boast of a Gothic basilica which barely escaped complete destruction, and of the pastels of Quentin de la Tour which are on display in the museum.

*In the flat country of Flanders, where the hard labour of men shows everywhere, and which is now divided between France and Belgium (opposite: beyond the belfry of Comines, the Lys, which is the border river), are proud cities which once throve on trade, and whose history can be read on the brick and stone of their fine, old houses. Below: the Place des Héros in Arras — an elegant flamboyant square with belfry, townhall, and arcaded houses.*

*Over fifty fortified churches stud the land of Thiérache like pious sentries, strong and crude, flanked by keeps, towers, and watch-turrets. Above: the church of Burelles (XVIth century), without a nave.*

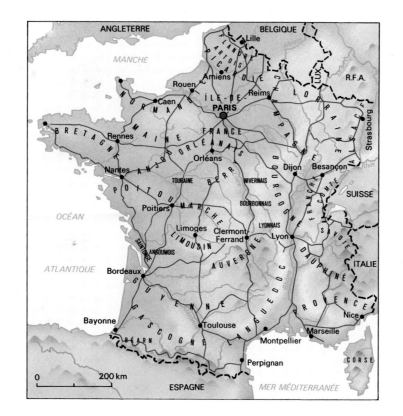

**Photographic credits**

*Pages 6 and 7 :* Mayer-Magnum, Perno-C.D. Tétrel. *Pages 8 and 9 :* R. Mazin. *Pages 10 and 11 :* Sappa-C.E.D.R.I., de Sazo-Rapho, R. Mazin. *Pages 12 and 13 :* Gabanou-Pictor-Aarons. *Pages 14 and 15 :* R. Mazin, R. Mazin, S. Marmounier. *Pages 16 and 17 :* Pictor-Aarons, R. Mazin. *Pages 18 and 19 :* G. Siöen-C.E.D.R.I., Sigard-Arepi. *Pages 20 and 21 :* G. Siöen-C.E.D.R.I, G. Siöen-C.E.D.R.I. *Pages 22 and 23 :* G. Siöen-C.E.D.R.I., G. Siöen-C.E.D.R.I. *Pages 24 and 25 :* A. Edouard-Studio des Gds-Augustins, Desjardins-Top. *Pages 26 and 27 :* E. Berne-Fotogram. *Pages 28 and 29 :* P. Hinous-Top, P. Hinous-Top, P. Tétrel. *Pages 30 and 31 :* R. Mazin-C.E.D.R.I., R. Mazin. *Pages 32 and 33 :* R. Mazin, P. Boulat-Sipa Press, P. Boulat-Sipa Press, P. Boulat-Sipa Press. *Pages 34 and 35 :* A. Edouard-Studio des Gds-Augustins. *Pages 36 and 37 :* Garanger-Sipa Press. *Pages 38 and 39 :* M. Garanger, K. Lawson-Rapho. *Pages 40 and 41 :* A. Weiss-Explorer, Rives-C.E.D.R.I. *Pages 42 and 43 :* Chapmann-Fotogram, S. Marmounier, A. Weiss-Explorer. *Pages 44 and 45 :* G. Sommer-Explorer. *Pages 46 and 47 :* Hinous-Top, Desjeux, Mayer-Magnum. *Pages 48 and 49 :* Hinous-Top, Desjeux-Tétrel. *Pages 50 and 51 :* P. Tétrel, M. Desjardins-Top. *Pages 52 and 53 :* Rives-C.E.D.R.I. *Pages 54 and 55 :* M. Desjardins-Top. *Pages 56 and 57 :* M. Desjardins-Top. *Pages 58 and 59 :* Rives-C.E.D.R.I. *Pages 60 and 61 :* Doisneau-Rapho, Doisneau-Rapho, Lauros-Giraudon. *Pages 62 and 63 :* H. Veiller-Explorer, S. Marmounier. *Pages 64 and 65 :* A. Nadeau-Studio des Gds-Augustins. *Pages 66 and 67 :* A. Nadeau-Studio des Gds-Augustins, Boubat-Top. *Pages 68 and 69 :* G. Marineau-Top, G. Marineau-Top. *Pages 70 and 71 :* G. Loucel-Fotogram, E. Mistler-Vloo, E. Mistler-Vloo. *Pages 72 and 73 :* P. Tétrel. *Pages 74 and 75 :* G. Siöen-C.E.D.R.I., C. Délu-Explorer. *Pages 76 and 77 :* J.-J. Arcis-Rapho, J.-J. Arcis-Rapho. *Pages 78 and 79 :* S. Marmounier, J. Gaillard-Top, C. Michel-Explorer. *Pages 80 and 81 :* S. Chirol, G. Martin-Guillou-C.D. Tétrel, J. J. Arcis-Rapho. *Pages 82 and 83 :* S. Chirol. *Pages 84 and 85 :* P. Tétrel, J.-Y. Derrien. *Pages 86 and 87 :* G. Siöen-C.E.D.R.I. *Pages 88 and 89 :* S. Chirol, G. Peress-Magnum. *Pages 90 and 91 :* Charbonnier-Top, P. Tétrel, Charbonnier-Top. *Pages 92 and 93 :* H. Chapmann-Fotogram, H. Chapmann-Fotogram, H. Chapmann-Fotogram. *Pages 94 and 95 :* W. Ronis-Rapho, L. Clergue. *Pages 96 and 97 :* M. Fraudreau-Top, M. Fraudreau-Top. *Pages 98 and 99 :* F. Jalin-C.E.D.R.I, W. Ronis-Rapho. *Pages 100 and 101 :* Silvester-Rapho. *Pages 102 and 103 :* Kalicanin-C.D. Tétrel, Dupont-Explorer, Loirat-C.D. Tétrel. *Pages 104 and 105 :* Loirat-C.D. Tétrel. *Pages 106 and 107 :* Briolle-Rapho, Loirat-C.D. Tétrel. *Pages 108 and 109 :* S. Marmounier, Duboutin-Explorer, C. Rives-C.E.D.R.I. *Pages 110 and 111 :* F. Jalain-C.E.D.R.I. *Pages 112 and 113 :* P. Tétrel, P. Tétrel. *Pages 114 and 115 :* P. Tétrel. *Pages 116 and 117 :* M. Desjardins-Top, P. Tétrel. *Pages 118 and 119 :* T. Vogel-Explorer. *Pages 120 and 121 :* M. Desjardins-Top, Binois-Pitch. *Pages 122 and 123 :* Bouillot-Marco-Polo, M. Delaborde. *Pages 124 and 125 :* Loirat-C.D. Tétrel, Zimmermann C.D.M.O. *Pages 126 and 127 :* R. Tixador-Top. *Pages 128 and 129 :* Loirat-C.D. Tétrel, Loirat-C.D. Tétrel. *Pages 130 and 131 :* S. Marmounier, M. Desjardins-Top, S. Marmounier. *Pages 132 and 133 :* M. Desjardins-Top, M. Desjardins-Top. *Pages 134 and 135 :* J. J. Arcis-Rapho. *Pages 136 and 137 :* H. Chapmann-Fotogram, G. Rébuffat. *Pages 138 and 139 :* G. and M. C. Papigny, Berne-Fotogram, Mandery-C.E.D.R.I. *Pages 140 and 141 :* B. Barbey-Magnum, J. Verroust. *Pages 142 and 143 :* Lepage-Vloo, B. Barbey-Magnum. *Pages 144 and 145 :* Sappa-C.E.D.R.I. *Page 147 :* F. Jalain, Bouquignaud-Top. *Pages 148 and 149 :* F. Jalain, P. Boulat-Sipa-Press. *Pages 150 and 151 :* Laiter-Vloo, P. Boulat-Sipa-Press, J. Bottin. *Pages 152 and 153 :* Anderson-Fournier-Explorer, J. Nosari. *Pages 154 and 155 :* J. Nosari, J. Nosari. *Pages 156 and 157 :* J. N. Reichel-Top, Leclercq-Fotogram, M. Cambazard-Explorer. *Page 158 :* M. Cambazard-Explorer.

*Map :* D. Horvath.

*Montcornet church almost entirely rebuilt after burning in 1574.*

Imprimerie Mame – Tours – septembre 1983. – Dépôt légal septembre 1983. – N° Éditeur 12015 – 523104 A Février 1984.
Imprimé en France *(Printed in France)*.